Beyond our Tears

Resources for times of remembrance

Prepared by the Joint Liturgical Group and
Churches Together in Britain and Ireland

Edited by Jean M. Mayland

CHURCHES TOGETHER
IN BRITAIN AND IRELAND

Churches Together in Britain and Ireland
Bastille Court
2 Paris Garden
London
SE1 8ND

Direct Line: +44 (0)207 654 7254
Fax: +44 (0)207 654 7222
www.ctbi.org.uk

ISBN 0 85169 286 9

Published 2004 by Churches Together in Britain and Ireland

Produced by Church House Publishing

Copyright © Churches Together in Britain and Ireland

Further copies available from
CTBI Publications
4 John Wesley Road, Peterborough PE4 6ZP, UK
Tel: + 44 (0)1733 325002; Fax: +44 (0)1733 384180
orders@ctbi.org.uk; sales@mph.org.uk

Cover design by Church House Publishing
Printed by Creative Print and Design Group, Ebbw Vale, Wales

Contents

Solemn the drums thrill; Death august and royal
Sings sorrows up into immortal spheres.
There is music in the midst of desolation
And a glory that shines upon our tears.

Laurence Binyon

Lord, we give you thanks for the gift of tears:
For tears of grief, redeeming our mourning from despair;
For tears of anger, awakening our thirst for justice;
For tears of laughter, celebrating our joy in living.

May the light of Christ shining through our tears
Become the rainbow of your promise,
Shedding colours of your love's bright presence
In your grieving, struggling, laughing world.

Author unknown

Preface

By the General Secretary of CTBI

This book has its origins in work that is still continuing to produce a new official service for Remembrance in association with The Royal British Legion. That service will be published in late summer 2005, and will be used for the first time at Remembrance services that year.

In the course of the preparation of this service it was suggested that a collection of resources concerning past conflicts, together with prayers for peace, justice and reconciliation, would be helpful to the Churches. The concept grew when the then Presidents of CTBI suggested that material should also be provided for other times of national and community grief and remembrance. Any act of Christian worship on such occasions will give grief its proper place, but it will also contain a note of hope. Hence the title: these resources are intended to help us move 'beyond our tears' to a place where hope and healing are to be found.

I am confident that this book will prove helpful to local churches and to 'Churches Together' Groups. Thanks are due to all those who have worked hard to produce this collection, particularly the editor, Jean Mayland, the members of the Joint Liturgical Group and those representatives of member Churches of CTBI who met and worked on the early drafts.

David Goodbourn
General Secretary
Churches Together in Britain and Ireland

Foreword

By the Chairman of the Joint Liturgical Group

At the heart of Christian worship is the call to remember: to remember who God is and where God has been in our lives and in the whole of history. It is there too in the very call of Christ, 'Do this in remembrance of me' (1 Corinthians 11.26). Remembrance is thus part of the very fibre of our Christian being, as well as being a vital part of our shared human experience. That is why these resources have been produced, in response to requests from many quarters. They are offered to the Churches to help in the process of remembering all that others have done and given by their courage, their witness and their very lives.

In that remembering we celebrate the gifts that we now enjoy and treasure, gifts of freedom, justice, peace and truth. Thus the past that we remember allows us to value ever more deeply the present in which we live. Our prayer of thanksgiving for the past and the present demands, then, our commitment to build a future that is rooted deeply in all we have celebrated by our remembering. From our group of liturgists across the Christian Churches this work has evolved in cooperation with many other individuals and groups, all of whom deserve our gratitude. It continues the fine tradition of remembering that has been part of our society for so many years. We now offer it to the wider world so that we may indeed do what God asks, in remembrance of Christ and of those who gave as he gave for the sake of others.

Monsignor Kevin McGinnell
Chair, Joint Liturgical Group (GB)
and English Language Liturgical Consultation

Acknowledgements

Our warm thanks go to Monsignor Kevin McGinnell, Mr Andrew Barr and other members of the Joint Liturgical Group for their hard work over a number of years and for their perseverance and patience. We are grateful for the work of the representatives of member Churches of CTBI from the four nations, who met at the Focolare Centre in January 2003 and worked hard on the Service of Reflection and Reconciliation and the Resources. We thank the Bishop of Manchester and The Royal British Legion most sincerely for their cooperation. We appreciate very much the help and advice given to us by the Revd Colin G. McIntosh, the Minister of Dunblane Cathedral, and the Revd Tim Alban Jones, the Vicar of Soham.

We thank the Minister and Vestry of Dunblane Cathedral, the Dean and Chapter of St Paul's Cathedral, London, and the Dean and Chapter of Southwark Cathedral for permission to use extracts from services held in their cathedrals.

We thank the following for permission to use material for which they hold copyright. Every effort has been made to trace and contact copyright holders. If there are any inadvertent omissions we apologize to those concerned and will ensure that a suitable acknowledgement is made at the next reprint.

The authors and the original publishers for the following poems: 'In Flanders Field', John McCrae; 'Christ in Flanders', Lucy Whitmell; 'The dead', Rupert Brooke; 'Asleep', 'Move him into the sun', and 'At a Calvary near Ancre', Wilfred Owen; 'For sleep or death', Ruth Pitter; 'The absent', Edwin Muir; 'High flight', Pilot Officer John Gillespie Magee Jr., 'Turn again to life', A. Price Hughes; The Society of Authors for permission to include 'For the fallen' by Laurence Binyon.

The Revd Tim Alban Jones for the extract from his address given at the memorial service in Ely Cathedral for Jessica Chapman and Holly Wells.

The Archbishops' Council of the Church of England for the collect beginning 'Almighty Father, whose will it is'; for the Act of Thanksgiving from The Promise of His Glory, Church House

Publishing, 1991; for 'A General Thanksgiving'; for 'Prayers for
those who have suffered from war'; for 'Prayers for peace'; for
'Prayers for the dead and those who mourn'; and for 'O Father
of all, we pray to you for those whom we love, But see no longer'
from Common Worship: Services and Prayers for the Church
of England, *Church House Publishing, 2000.*

The Revd Alan Ashton for extracts from his reflection on the
agonizing events in Soham, which first appeared in Pilgrim
Post, *Issue 73, February 2003, published by Churches Together
in England.*

Mrs Iris Bagnall for permission to use her husband's description
of the Falklands War, from his book Faith under Fire, *published
by Marshall Morgan & Scott in 1983.*

Alice Bold, who holds the copyright for the poem 'Cause and
effect' by her husband, Alan Bold.

BBC News Online for 'The Husband's story' and 'The Mother's story'.

The Revd Dr Derek Browning for the prayer 'Lord, there are
times when prayer is hard work'.

The Church of Scotland Panel on Worship for the prayers
beginning 'Gracious God', 'Lord God, fear comes in many guises
into our lives', 'We pray for all afflicted in the tradgedy in . . .',
'Lord, there are times when I am worn out with grief', and 'Lord,
why me? Why this? Why now?'

The Cathedral of St Paul the Apostle, Los Angeles, for the Litany
of Remembrance.

The Continuum International Publishing Group for the prayer
'Eternal God' from Celebrating Common Prayer *by the Society
of St Francis.*

The Dean and Chapter of Coventry Cathedral for permission to
use the Coventry Cathedral Litany of Reconciliation.

Monsignor Gerry Fitzpatrick for the music to The Lord's Prayer,
'Forgive us, Lord, our lamps are faint' and the Song of Farewell
'Receive his/her soul'.

Kathy Galloway for her two poems 'Let us be different' and 'There will be peace between us', for which she holds copyright. First published in Love Burning Deep, *SPCK, 1993; to be reissued in Kathy Galloway,* The Dream of Learning Our True Name, *Wild Goose Publications, 2004.*

Jean Holloway for the hymn 'O Father on your love we call'.

Fleur Houston for the text of her hitherto unpublished 'Affirmation'.

The Independent *newspaper for permission to reprint the extracts from the obituary of the Revd Kenneth Hayes by Iain McLean published on 31 January 1998.*

The International Committee on English in the Liturgy (Inc) for the English translation of the Opening Prayer from the English translation of the Roman Missal © *1973; excerpts from the English translation of* The Roman Missal *©1973; the English translation of the Penitential Rite (Form C) from* The Roman Missal *©1973 and excerpts from the English translation of the* Order of Christian Funerals © *1985.*

Donald Macaskill for the poems 'It cannot' and 'Madrid Madness'.

Margaret Thatcher Foundation for the extract from The Downing Street Years *and margaretthatcher.org, the official web site of the Foundation, first published by HarperCollins, 1993.*

Kevin Mayhew Ltd for the music by Martin Morran to 'You raise the dead', and the words and music of Psalm 129 and 'How blest are those who have died' © Noel S. Donnelly.

Methodist Publishing House for 'Thanks for true peace', © John Johansen-Berg, first published in The Way of Peace, *ed. Hannah Ward.*

Janet Morley for the 'Psalm of grief' and the prayer 'O God who brought us to birth'.

James Murdoch Ewing for his poem 'For Armistice Day', first published in Life and Work.

Random House Group for extracts from Forgotten Stories of the Great War *by Max Arthur, published by Ebury Press (Sergeant*

Thomas Painting, Sergeant Jack Dorgan, Private W. Underwood and Kitty Eckersley) and for the extract from Remembrance *by Theresa Breslin published by Doublesday.*

Godfrey Rust for the reading from the poem 'September 1, 2001', first read in St John's Church, Ealing, 16 September 2001, © Geoffrey Rust, Wordsout Publications, 14 Gloucester Road, London W5 4JB; email: godfrey@wordsout.co.uk.

The Revd Andrew Scobie for 'A prayer for unity, peace and justice'.

The Revd Dr Paul Sheppy for 'A prayer for those who suffer'; 'A prayer for a schoolfriend who has been killed'; 'A prayer for a murder victim'; and 'A prayer for the victim of an accident'.

Stainer and Bell, London, for 'Say "no" to peace' by Brian Wren © 1986.

The West Yorkshire Ecumenical Council for the Second World War stories of 'The Daughter', 'The Dancer', and 'The Tailor' from From War to Peace: Recollections and Reflections 1945–1995 from Leeds, Dortmund, Buffalo, Amiens, Zwickau, *published 1995.*

Wild Goose Publications, the Iona Community and Donald McIlhagga for the poem 'The way to peace' by Kate McIlhagga, from Lent and Easter Readings from Iona, *ed. Neil Paynter, 2002 and republished in May 2004 in a retrospective collection entitled* The Green Heart of the Snowdrop.

Wild Goose Publications, The Iona Community for the 'Affirmation of faith by two 14-year-old boys'; Wild Goose Resource Group, the Iona Community for the Assurance beginning 'The desert will sing and rejoice', from the Iona Abbey Worship Book; *for the hymn 'We cannot measure how you heal', from* When grief is raw *(Wild Goose Publications, 1997), words by John L. Bell and Graham Maule, music: 'Ye banks and braes', Scottish trad. (copyright words and arrangement ©1989,1996,WGRG, Iona Community, Glasgow G2 3DH); and for 'What shall we pray' from* When grief is raw *(as before), words by Carnwadric Parish Church Worship Group and John L.Bell, music: Kingston, John L. Bell (copyright words and arrangement © 1989,1996, WGRG, Iona Community, as before).*

Acknowledgements

Woodlake Books for the ceremony of the candles which forms the Act of Remembrance in the service of Reflection and Reconciliation; for the prayer of sending out beginning 'Go forth'; and for the affirmation beginning 'I believe God made the world' from Seasons of the Spirit – Congregational Life 2002–2003.

The World Council of Churches for the prayer 'Eternal God, whose image lies in the heart of all people', from the Vancouver Assembly Worship Book, 1983.

Zondervan Corporation for the prayer 'Remembrance' by Kate Compston, from Dare to Dream, *ed.* Geoffrey Duncan, 1995 © Council for World Mission *and for the extract from* Marie: A Story from Enniskillen *by Gordon Wilson and Alf McCleary.*

The source of the poem 'The gift of tears' is unknown.

Background to this Book

This book has come into existence in response to distinct but related requests. The original initiative came from the Millennium Group of Churches Together in England, which suggested the time was right for some revision of the traditional Remembrance services. Since the services are used across the whole United Kingdom, it was to Churches Together in Britain and Ireland (CTBI) that the request was remitted. After consultation with CTBI member Churches, and in particular at the suggestion of the Church of England, the task of preparing new material was remitted to one of CTBI's Networks, the Joint Liturgical Group (JLG). Much work has been done by that group and progress has been made in new structures and ideas for the keeping of Remembrance each November.

By virtue of the terms of its Royal Charter, however, the custodian of the nation's Remembrance is The Royal British Legion (the Legion). That body has expressed the view that the appropriate time for the publication of an official new service would be late summer 2005 for use at the Remembrance Services in November 2005 and thereafter. This would allow for due observation to be given to the Sixtieth Anniversary of D Day Commemorations in 2004 and the special VE/VJ Day commemorations on 10 July 2005. CTBI is happy to concur with this advice and such a service will be published in late summer 2005 and will be available in pamphlet form.

During the last five years, alongside work on the new service, a considerable amount of work has been done by the JLG to provide additional resources (stories, poems, prayers etc.) for use at times of Remembrance of past conflicts. During this period the Presidents of CTBI discussed the progress of the work at one of their regular meetings. At that time, they added a new request – that the new material should also take account of other causes of widespread public grief. They had in mind accidents causing many casualties, terrorist bombings and tragic events like the shootings at Dunblane. This request was also taken up by CTBI and the JLG.

It has been agreed by CTBI, JLG and the Legion that it would be helpful to publish all this resource material at this time. The first section of this book contains useful material for the Remembrance of those who have given their lives in past conflicts, poems of reflection and prayers for justice and peace. It ends with a service entitled 'Blessed are the peace makers', which suggests a fresh way of praying for peace.

The second section of this book is a collection of material drawn together to meet the request of the CTBI Presidents. Much of this material was offered by representatives of member Churches of CTBI. Valuable help was also given by the Revd Colin G. McIntosh, the Minister of Dunblane Cathedral, and the Revd Tim Alban Jones, the Vicar of Soham. This collection is a first response to the request of the Presidents. The Joint Liturgical Group intends to do much deeper theological work on the phenomena of the expressions of popular grief and to prepare new material in the light of their study.

In preparing the material for the book CTBI consulted widely. A residential consultation, representative of England, Wales, Scotland and Northern Ireland, responded actively to the first draft. Each CTBI member Church was then invited to comment, and their comments were given very careful attention. In its final form, the collection is now offered as a resource, which it is hoped will prove useful in a wide variety of ways and on numerous occasions.

Remembrance

It is important for people to remember and celebrate our past as it roots us in who we are and what is important about our national identity. Remembrance, however, is not just about the past. In the Jewish tradition, at a Festival such as the Passover, the past is recalled, through the telling of the story, so that it may become real and alive in the present and be effective in encouraging and directing life in the future. In the Christian Eucharist, and particularly in the Eucharistic prayer, the saving acts of God in Creation and Redemption through Christ are recalled in such a way that we may be reconciled with God and share in the divine life here and eternally.

The observation of Remembrance Sunday should have within it those elements of recalling, reliving, reconciling, rededication and hope for the future. People need to be helped to remember the horrors of war and the heroism of individuals through story, music and silence, so that these may become real in the present and influence and inspire us to work for reconciliation, peace and justice in the future. We believe that the structure, the wording and the symbolic actions of services should facilitate this process. Help may need to be given to assist people in using the Two Minute Silence in a creative way, i.e. recalling, reliving and recommitting in hope.

Other important concepts

At Remembrance time words and concepts which are important to Christians and particularly dear to the Legion come to the fore. Examples of these would be duty, sacrifice, loyalty, responsibility and seeking the common good. They would also include the Legion's five values of Reflection, Hope, Comradeship, Selflessness and Service, which are basic values that can help to bind people together. Remembrance time is a good moment to seek to reaffirm them in the life of society. Nevertheless this needs to be done with sensitivity so as not to put off those to whom they may be less familiar and who may react against them. While seeking to affirm values we hope may be common to all, Remembrance Services should never seek merely to express the lowest common denominator. It is important that they retain their religious dimension.

The Royal British Legion

Britain's first poppy day was held in 1921, the year The British Legion (now The Royal British Legion) was founded to seek to safeguard the welfare, interests and memory of ex-Service people and their dependants. The Legion is the largest provider of welfare for ex-Service people. A British Legion Service was first broadcast from the Cenotaph on Whitsunday 1928 and the silence was first broadcast from the Cenotaph on 11 November 1928. For many years now the BBC has broadcast and shown on television the service at the Cenotaph, on the second Sunday in November, and the march past by veterans, which follows. The Bishop of London always conducts the service, in his capacity as Dean of the Chapel Royal. The service is traditional in style although it has changed gradually over the years.

On the Saturday evening before the Cenotaph Service, The Royal British Legion Festival of Remembrance takes place in the Royal Albert Hall in the presence of members of the Royal Family. This also ends with a service of worship, whose liturgical style is evolving, which is conducted by the National Chaplain of The Royal British Legion.

In some towns and villages, members of the Legion attend Remembrance services at the cenotaph or in the local church. On these occasions local Ministers have an opportunity to introduce new material but it would be helpful to consult the Legion.

The Two Minute Silence

In recent years the Legion have revived the practice of observing the Two Minute Silence on 11 November. This has been well observed by a general public now affected by events such as the Dunblane massacre and 11 September. The intention was to encourage all people – of all faiths and of none – simply to remember and resolve to seek peace in the two minutes they kept silence, wherever they were. Those involved in worship on the second Sunday in November also observe the Two Minute Silence as part of the Act of Remembrance during the service. Christian people should value both opportunities to keep silence. It is, however, particularly important to teach the Christian concepts of remembrance which we might wish to encourage during the silence as it is observed during worship services.

Other faith communities

In a multi cultural Britain, the issue of the involvement of people of other faiths in the observance of Remembrance is an important one. For some years now, the Jewish Community have held their own service at the Cenotaph in London. Consideration is being given nationally to appropriate ways of reflecting multi faith Britain including commemoration of those of the world's great faiths who have given their lives in Britain's Armed Services. Within this book people of other faiths are remembered in stories and prayers.

Who are remembered?

Remembrance Day began as a day on which to remember the dead of the First World War. A few of these old comrades still

survive but the number decreases each year and soon there will
be memories and stories but no living people. In time the dead
of the Second World War were added to those remembered, and
gradually those who have died in more recent conflicts such as
those in Northern Ireland, Korea, the Falklands, the Gulf War and
the war in Iraq have been remembered. There has, in fact, been
only one year since 1945 in which no one was killed on active
service. This was 1968. In recent years groups such as the land
army and civilian emergency services of the Second World
War have claimed their right to be included in the Act of
Remembrance and the subsequent march past, and in some
ways the list is increasing and not decreasing.

Peace-keeping and making

The British Armed Forces today increasingly have a role in
peace-keeping and need our prayers. They are our representatives
and have a vicarious role on behalf of the whole community.
This element needs to be brought into our Remembrance Services.
Such services should never be occasions to glorify war but could
increasingly become occasions, which value and encourage peace
making and the search for justice.

Jean Mayland

Remembering Past Conflicts: Looking Forward in Hope

Worship material,
stories and poems

A Suggested Shape for a
Service of Remembrance

In the introduction to this collection of material it is stated that
the structure, the wording and the symbolic actions of the service
should facilitate the process of remembrance. We suggest below
a possible structure, and the resources which follow give examples
of the kind of material which might be used within this structure.
They can of course also be used completely independently.

Gathering
Welcome and statement of purpose
Prayers of penitence
Collect
Proclaiming and receiving the Word
Praying – thanksgiving and interceding
Remembrance
Pledging
Personal commitment
Affirmation of faith
(*If a Eucharist is celebrated it continues here with
the taking of the bread and wine.*)
Sending out
Prayer
National Anthem
Blessing

In all services and prayers in this book, the words of any prayers
printed in **bold** type are intended to be spoken by all present.

A Plea for Forgiveness

Minister
> All have sinned and fall short of the glory of God.
>
> The hatred which divides nation from nation,
> race from race, class from class,
> **Father Forgive.**
>
> The covetous desires of people and nations
> to possess what is not their own,
> **Father Forgive.**
>
> The greed which exploits the work of human hands
> and lays waste the earth,
> **Father Forgive.**
>
> Our envy of the welfare and happiness of others,
> **Father Forgive.**
>
> Our indifference to the imprisoned, the homeless,
> the refugee,
> **Father Forgive.**
>
> The lust which dishonours the bodies of men,
> women and children,
> **Father Forgive.**
>
> The pride which leads to trust in ourselves
> and not in God,
> **Father Forgive.**
>
> Be kind to one another, tender-hearted,
> forgiving one another,
> as God in Christ forgives you.
> **Amen.**

Coventry Cathedral Litany of Reconciliation

A Declaration of the Mercy of God

Lord Jesus, you came to gather the nations into
the peace of the Kingdom of God.
Lord, have mercy.
Lord, have mercy.

Lord Jesus, you come in word and sacrament
to make your people strong.
Christ, have mercy.
Christ, have mercy.

Lord Jesus, you will come in glory, with salvation
for all your people.
Lord, have mercy.
Lord, have mercy.

Roman Catholic Missal

Collects and Suggested Readings

Collects

Almighty Father,
whose will is to restore all things
in your beloved Son, the King of all:
govern the hearts and minds of those in authority,
and bring the families of the nations,
divided and torn apart by the ravages of sin,
to be subject to his just and gentle rule;
who is alive and reigns with you,
in the unity of the Holy Spirit,
one God, now and for ever.
Amen.

Common Worship

or

Eternal God,
in whose perfect realm
no sword is drawn but the sword of justice,
and no strength known but the strength of love:
guide and inspire all who seek your kingdom,
that peoples and nations may find their security
in the love which casts out fear;
through Jesus Christ our Saviour.
Amen.

Celebrating Common Prayer

or

God of power and mercy,
you destroy war and put down earthly pride.
Banish violence from our midst and wipe away our tears
that we may deserve to be called your sons and daughters.
We ask this through our Lord Jesus Christ, your Son,
who lives and reigns with you and the Holy Spirit,
one God, for ever and ever.
Amen.

Roman Catholic Missal

Proclaiming and receiving the Word

The readings may be taken from the Common Lectionary of the Sunday, or special lessons for Remembrance may be used as set out below for the three-year lectionary.

Old Testament reading

Year A: Isaiah 25.1-9
Year B: Deuteronomy 4.9-14 or Isaiah 52.7-12
Year C: Micah 4.1-8

Psalm

Year A: Psalm 20
Response:
**May the Lord hear you in the day of trouble:
the name of the God of Jacob defend you.**

Year B: Psalm 46
Response:
**God is our refuge and strength,
a very present help in trouble.**

Year C: Psalm 9.9-20.
Response:
The Lord makes himself known by his acts of justice.

New Testament reading

Year A: Revelation 22.1-5
Year B: Romans 8.31-39
Year C: 2 Thessalonians 2.13-3.5 or Revelation 21.1-6a

Gospel

Year A: St Matthew 5.1-12 or 5.38-48
Year B: St John 15.9-17
Year C: St Luke 1.68-79
Readings from the Methodist Sunday Service Book and/or the Church of Scotland Book of Common Order

Stories of War and Reconciliation

The First World War

Sergeant Thomas Painting, 1st Battalion, King's Royal Rifle Corps
At the battle of the Aisne we got over the river and onto the high ground over a mile in front of the Aisne. We knew there was about a brigade of Jerries against us and we were only seven platoons. During the fight we got pushed back about 300 yards; we had to leave our wounded and our dead. The Highland Light Infantry and Worcesters came up. Private Wilson of the HLI and one of our men attacked a machine-gun. Our man got killed but Private Wilson killed the machine-gunner and captured the position and got the Victoria Cross. Our man got a wooden cross. That's the difference, you see. One killed – one a Victoria Cross.

Sergeant Jack Dorgan, 7th Battalion, Northumberland Fusiliers
Private Bob Young was conscious right to the last. I lay alongside of him and said, 'Can I do anything for you, Bob?' He said, 'Straighten my legs, Jack' – but he had no legs. I touched the bones, and that satisfied him. Then he said: 'Get my wife's photograph out of my breast pocket.' I took the photograph and put it in his hands. He couldn't move, he couldn't lift a hand, he couldn't lift a finger, but somehow he held his wife's photo on his chest. And that is how Bob Young died.

Private W. Underwood, 1st Canadian Division
I was given seven days' Number 1 Field Punishment, which consists of being tied on a wagon wheel. You're spread-eagled with the hub of the wheel in your back, and your legs and wrists handcuffed to the wheel. You'd do two hours up and four hours down for seven days, day and night. And the cold! It was January 1915, a really cold month, and when they took you down they had to rub you to get the circulation going in your limbs again. And the only reason I was there was because I missed a roll call.

Kitty Eckersley
When I found out that I was pregnant I went to see them at the leather works and they said they would find me some light work. So I had a very nice job and worked there until I was seven months pregnant.

I didn't go out much because I had a very bad time during my pregnancy – the only thing I could keep in my stomach was carrots. They were cheap, so I had two pounds of carrots every day. I was very thin at the time.

My mother had a little job picking strawberries at a jam factory, so there was only me in the house when I heard the postman come. I knew there would be a letter for me, so I ran down in my nightdress and opened the door, snatched the letter off him and ran in and shut the door again. I opened the letter and saw it was from his sergeant. It just said: 'I'm very sorry to tell you of the death of your husband.' Well, that was as far as I could read. I don't really know what happened over the next few minutes, but I must have run out of my house as I was, in my bare feet, and banged on the next door. They brought some blankets and wrapped me up in them and sent for my mother, so she came home and treated me for shock. His letter was only from his sergeant, so I thought perhaps it was an error. So later on I wrote back to the sergeant, but I had another letter to say that he also had been killed. Then, later on, I got the official news.

The Second World War

The Daughter

It starts with my grandfather who lost his arm in World War I and his son in World War II. He was my 'father figure' and a constant reminder of war and its effects upon people and families. He always said that losing his arm was the best thing that happened to him – he was invalided out of the Army, was able to set up his own market stall and eventually a small shop, before the flood of men came looking for jobs in 1918. And he always had his pension to supplement his income. In the end, though, it was having no arm that killed him – he missed his footing and fell from a bus when he was 90.

So I was aware of the effects of war even before I was old enough to know that my own father had died at Arnhem – when in September 1944 he was shot down and his parachute didn't open. I was born in January 1945. My mother did not have the confirmation of my father's death until VE Day [8 May 1945]. As everyone else celebrated, her loss was proved. My grandfather, he never attended church after World War II and never spoke to me about his beliefs . . . The effects of war are still present in our family.

The Dancer
I still remember Friday, 14 March.

That evening we were in the Lyceum cinema when the siren sounded. We walked home to our back-to-back. Bombers were overhead, so we went into the cellar. Just after midnight Mum felt poorly; we returned to the living-room. My sister and I went upstairs to fetch some blankets and called, 'Leeds is on fire!' We came down and a bomb crashed through the chimney. I was trapped in rubble and covered with soot. My legs were burning. My boyfriend tried to pull me away from the fireplace. My sister called out and lost consciousness. I was conscious and remember intense pain.

The rescue workers took us outside – it was cold – then to a neighbour's house. The ambulance arrived and took us to the Infirmary. Next day my uncle realized Mum had not been rescued. He dug her body out of the rubble.

My sister and I were so ill. We were told of Mum's death three weeks later. My brother heard about the bomb just before he was taken prisoner by the Japanese. I remember weeks of pain . . . Eventually the surgeon decided to amputate my right leg just below the knee . . . When discharged, I hopped on crutches, on and off buses, carrying shopping.

In 1942 I met my husband. In December 1942 I got my first artificial leg. We were married in January 1943 and lived in Quarry Hill Flats, where I was to pull our son (born 1944) and his pushchair up 45 steps. Our other two sons were born in the prefabs at Beckett Park.

Since 1941 I have smiled and danced through life, winning medals for ballroom and Latin-American dancing in 1981.

The Tailor
I was only 21 and recently married when the war started. My husband was drafted into the tank regiment a few months after we were married and I spent the war years making army, naval and air-force uniforms. I lived five minutes away from the

nearest air raid shelter. As soon as the sirens rang out I would wrap up blankets, pillow and food, and run as fast as I could to the shelter. Everyone shared their food and drink, and sang, and as soon as the sirens rang out again with the all-clear we would all go home . . .

My family suffered as many others in different countries all over the world. I had eight fit brothers at the start of the war. At the end, one was killed in Burma; one lost an eye when a Bren gun backfired; one lost his hearing when a horse kicked him in the head; and one was invalided out when his wife committed suicide by throwing herself out of the bedroom window.

The war was a time of sorrow, but great comradeship existed and everyone shared what they had.

Reconciliation in Khatyn among European women
The people of Byelorussia (now Belarus) suffered intensely in the Second World War, which they refer to as the Great Patriotic War. As the Germans conquered, they followed a deliberate policy of extermination of the people. In the event more than three-quarters of the population survived, but even so 2,230,000 people died during those terrible years.

In October 1987 the members of the Coordinating Committee of the Ecumenical Forum of European Christian Women visited the site of Khatyn, one of the villages whose entire population had been exterminated. Khatyn was a small village of 26 households, protected against the winds by white birch trees and tall pines. It was neat and cosy, with its shaduf wells and thick lilac bushes in the front gardens. On 22 March 1943 the life of Khatyn came to an end. A detachment of soldiers entered the village and drove all the inhabitants into a barn, to which they set fire. When some of the people trapped inside battered down the door and tried to escape, they were mown down by machine-gun fire. One hundred and forty-nine people were exterminated, among them seventy-five children. Only one man survived.

Today a great marble slab covers the communal grave of the villagers; the gigantic black statue of a father, the one man who escaped, stands dwarfing the landscape, as for ever he holds his dead child in his arms. On the site of each chimney in the ruins of each house of Khatyn there now stands a small bell tower;

constantly, in sequence, mourning bells ring out, each one a
memorial to a different village that was destroyed and never
rebuilt. A Wall of Life commemorates, in metal names, all the
villages that were rebuilt. A long row of niches bears the names
of concentration camps in which thousands of people died in
agony. Before a black memorial slab the Eternal Flame burns.
The group of women walked slowly round, stopping at three
places to pray and sing and lay red carnations. At the end the
West German woman in the party stood before the Eternal Flame
in tears. She felt the guilt of the whole German nation on her
German shoulders. It was the Russian woman who went to her,
put her arms round her, and said, 'Don't cry; don't blame yourself.
That is history. What we must make sure of now is that it never
happens again. We must work for peace.'

As a result of the initiative of the German woman, the Ecumenical
Forum of European Christian Women now runs a number of
projects in Belarus for children who suffer as a result of the
Chernobyl nuclear disaster.

Jean Mayland

The Falklands War

Sir Galahad
The landing ships, *Sir Tristram* and *Sir Galahad*, full of men,
equipment and munitions, had been sent round to Bluff Cove and
Fitzroy in preparation for the final assault on Port Stanley. The
clouds cleared while the ships were still unloading the Rapier
missiles which would protect them from an air attack and the
Argentinians scored hits on both. *Sir Galahad* had not discharged
its troops and the result was great loss of life and many survivors
were left with terrible burns. The Welsh Guards took the brunt of
it. As on all these occasions, the natural reaction was 'if only' –
above all, if only the men had been taken off and dispersed as
soon as they arrived then nothing like this number of casualties
would have been suffered. But the losses would have been even
greater were it not for the heroism of the helicopter pilots. They
hovered close to the burning oil slicks around the ship and used
the draughts from their rotors to blow life rafts full of survivors
away from the inferno into which they were being drawn.

Margaret Thatcher

The Residents of Port Stanley

But the initial excitement we had felt over the shelling, the surge of expectation at each *whoosh* and *crunch*, had given way to a constant sorrow at the deaths and woundings that were happening. It had been a long catalogue of grief that had brought us to this point – necessary, but no less grievous. The *Belgrano*, the loss of *Sheffield* and other ships, and the horror of *Sir Galahad* and *Sir Tristram* that very week had brought home to us the reality of war and the suffering it brings with it . . . That evening, the sadness came very close to the heart of our community . . . It had been a day of heavy action . . . At around midnight, tragedy struck. A number of people were sleeping in the house of John Fowler, the Education Superintendent, in Ross Road West. The Argentines were shelling Mount Longdon, and the British were returning fire. There was also a naval bombardment in progress. A shell fell not far beyond this house and exploded and another exploded a little way in front of the house. Shrapnel from the second shell entered the house and injured a number of people, two of whom died immediately. The third, an elderly lady of 82, Mary Goodwin, was seriously wounded. She died a little time afterwards, on the morning of the ceasefire. These three were the only residents of Port Stanley to die because of the invasion.

Harry Bagnall

The War in Iraq

The Husband's story

My wife, Jo, is an RAF doctor working as part of an aeromedical evacuation team. It's her job to look after casualties as they are being flown out of the war zones, back to safer locations.

Unfortunately, she is there to certify the dead too. She hasn't been needed that much, which is excellent. Meanwhile, I'm at home looking after our one-year-old son, Alexander.

I understand why she's gone, but it's very frustrating because my wife has missed her son's first birthday.

Jo has also missed watching her son starting to crawl and speak and get more teeth. That's probably the hardest bit.

I've had plenty of excellent support: from my parents, her parents, brothers and sisters.

But I don't think most people realize civilian husbands of military personnel exist. All the talk is of supporting 'our boys' at war, and I find that very frustrating. It's not just husbands that have gone out there; it's wives and mothers too.

This is the first time Jo's been away in a war zone, and during the combat I was constantly watching BBC News 24 and checking News Online.

That's the most heart-rending thing: just watching it on the news and wondering where she is and what she's doing and is she all right; is she coming back?

BBC Web Site

The Mother's story
My son was a junior officer in the Iraq Army. When I knew there was to be a war we were afraid for him. I did not want him to die in battle, but he said he had to go. He was afraid that if he didn't fight, people from the regime would take him away and execute him.

On 2 April we said goodbye to him.

He was sent to fight in the Al-Tarmiya region outside Baghdad.

That same night, someone from the hospital came and told us that our son had bled to death after being wounded in battle.

We don't think he was properly looked after in hospital. They just let him bleed to death.

Why did this happen? Will Mr Bush give us money to look after his two children now?

We are poor people, and I am so worried about the little ones' future. There is a girl of six and a boy aged three. Who will look after them?

My son's name was Diya Khalil. He was 37 years old.

BBC Web Site

Poems

In Flanders fields

In Flanders fields the poppies blow
Between the crosses, row on row
That mark our place; and in the sky
The larks, still bravely singing, fly
Scarce heard amid the guns below.

We are the Dead. Short days ago
We lived, felt dawn, saw sunset glow,
Loved and were loved, and now we lie
In Flanders fields.

Take up our quarrel with the foe:
To you from failing hands we throw
The torch; be yours to hold it high.
If ye break faith with us who die
We shall not sleep, though poppies grow
In Flanders fields.

John McCrae

For the fallen

With proud thanksgiving, a mother for her children,
England mourns for her dead across the sea.
Flesh of her flesh they were, spirit of her spirit,
Fallen in the cause of the free.

Solemn the drums thrill; Death august and royal
Sings sorrows up into immortal spheres.
There is music in the midst of desolation
And a glory that shines upon our tears.

They went with songs to the battle, they were young,
Straight of limb, true of eye, steady and aglow.
They were staunch to the end against odds uncounted,
They fell with their faces to the foe.

They shall grow not old, as we that are left grow old:
Age shall not weary them, nor the years condemn.
At the going down of the sun and in the morning
We will remember them.

They mingle not with their laughing comrades again;
They sit no more at familiar tables of home;
They have no lot in our labour of the day-time;
They sleep beyond England's foam.

But where our desires are and our hopes profound,
Felt as a well-spring that is hidden from sight,
To the innermost heart of their own land they are known
As the stars are known to the Night;

As the stars that shall be bright when we are dust,
Moving in marches upon the heavenly plain;
As the stars that are starry in the time of our darkness,
To the end, to the end, they remain.

Laurence Binyon

Christ in Flanders

We had forgotten You, or very nearly –
You did not seem to touch us very nearly –
Of course we thought about You now and then;
Especially in any time of trouble –
But we are very ordinary men.

And there were always other things to think of –
There's lots of things a man has got to think of –
His work, his home, his pleasure, and his wife;
And so we only thought of You on Sunday –
Sometimes, perhaps, not even on a Sunday –
Because there's always lots to fill one's life.

And, all the while, in street or lane or byway –
In country lane, in city street, or byway –
You walked among us, and we did not see.
Your feet were bleeding as You walked our pavements –
How *did* we miss Your footprints on our pavements? –
Can there be other folk as blind as we?

Now we remember; over here in Flanders –
(It isn't strange to think of You in Flanders) –
This hideous warfare seems to make things clear.
We never thought about You much in England –
But now that we are far away from England,
We have no doubts, we know that You are here.

You helped us pass the jest along the trenches –
Where, in cold blood, we waited in the trenches –
You touched its ribaldry and made it fine.
You stood beside us in our pain and weakness –
We're glad to think You understand our weakness –
Somehow it seems to help us not to whine.

We think about You kneeling in the Garden –
Ah! God! The agony of that dread Garden –
We know You prayed for us upon the cross.
If anything could make us glad to bear it –
'Twould be the knowledge that You willed to bear it –
Pain – death – the uttermost of human loss.

Though we forgot You – You will not forget us –
We feel so sure that You will not forget us –
But stay with us until this dream is past.
And so we ask for courage, strength, and pardon –
Especially, I think, we ask for pardon –
And that You'll stand beside us to the last.

Lucy Whitmell

The Dead

These hearts were woven of human joys and cares,
Washed marvellously with sorrow, swift to mirth.
The years had given them kindness. Dawn was theirs,
And sunset, and the colours of the earth.
These had seen movement, and heard music; known
Slumber and waking; loved; gone proudly friended;
Felt the quick stir of wonder; sat alone;
Touched flowers and furs and cheeks. All this is ended.

There are waters blown by changing winds to laughter
And lit by the rich skies, all day. And after,
Frost, with a gesture, stays the waves that dance
And wandering loveliness. He leaves a white
Unbroken glory, a gathered radiance,
A width, a shining peace, under the night.

Rupert Brooke

Asleep

Under his helmet, up against his pack,
After the many days of work and waking,
Sleep took him by the brow and laid him back.
And in the happy no-time of his sleeping,
Death took him by the heart. There was a quaking
Of the aborted life within him leaping . . .
Then chest and sleepy arms once more fell slack.
And soon the slow, stray blood came creeping
From the intrusive lead, like ants on track.

Whether his deeper sleep lie shaded by the shaking
Of great wings, and the thoughts that hung the stars,
High pillowed on calm pillows of God's making
Above these clouds, these rains, these sleets of lead,
And these winds' scimitars;
– Or whether yet his thin and sodden head
Confuses more and more with the low mould,
His hair being one with the grey grass
And finished fields of autumns that are old . . .
Who knows? Who hopes? Who troubles? Let it pass!
He sleeps. He sleeps less tremulous, less cold,
Than we who must awake, and waking say Alas!

Wilfred Owen

Futility

Move him into the sun –
Gently its touch awoke him once,
At home, whispering of fields unsown.
Always it woke him, even in France,
Until this morning and this snow.
If anything might rouse him now
The kind old sun will know.

Think how it wakes the seeds, –
Woke once the clays of a cold star.
Are limbs, so dear-achieved, are sides,
Full-nerved, still warm, too hard to stir?
Was it for this the clay grew tall?
– O what made fatuous sunbeams toil
To break earth's sleep at all?

At a Calvary near the Ancre

One ever hangs where shelled roads part.
In this war He too lost a limb,
But His disciples hide apart;
And now the Soldiers bear with Him.

Near Golgotha strolls many a priest,
And in their faces there is pride
That they were flesh-marked by the Beast
By whom the gentle Christ's denied.

The scribes on all the people shove
And brawl allegiance to the state,
But they who love the greater love
Lay down their life; they do not hate.

Two poems by Wilfred Owen: set by
Benjamin Britten in the War Requiem

For sleep, or death

Cure me with quietness,
Bless me with peace;
Comfort my heaviness,
Stay me with ease.
Stillness in solitude
Send down like dew;
Mine armour of fortitude
Piece and make new:
That when I rise again
I may shine bright
As the sky after rain,
Day after night.

Ruth Pitter

The absent

They are not here. And we, we are the Others
Who walk by ourselves unquestioned in the sun
Which shines for us and only for us.
For They are not here.
And are made known to us in this great absence
That lies upon us and is between us
Since They are not here.
Now, in this kingdom of summer idleness
Where slowly we the sun-tranced multitudes dream
    and wander
In deep oblivion of brightness
And breathe ourselves out, out into the air –
It is absence that receives us;
We do not touch, our souls go out in the absence
That lies between us and is about us.
For we are the Others,
And so we sorrow for These that are not with us,
Not knowing we sorrow or that this is our sorrow,
Since it is long past thought or memory or device
    of mourning,
Sorrow for loss of that which we never possessed,
The unknown, the nameless,
The ever-present that in their absence are with us
(With us the inheritors, the usurpers claiming
The sun and the kingdom of the sun) that sorrow
And loneliness might bring a blessing upon us.

                                        Edwin Muir

High flight

Oh! I have slipped the surly bonds of earth
And danced the skies on laughter-silvered wings:
Sunward I've climbed and joined the tumbling mirth
Of sun-split clouds – and done a hundred things
You have not dreamed of – wheeled and soared and swung
High in the sunlit silence. Hovering there
I've chased the shouting wind along, and flung
My eager craft through footless halls of air.
Up, up the long, delirious, burning blue
I've topped the wind-swept heights with easy grace,
Where never lark or even eagle flew;

And while with silent lifting mind I've trod
The high untrespassed sanctity of space,
Put out my hand and touched the face of God.

Pilot Officer John Gillespie Magee Jr

Cause and effect

He thought before the war
Of conflicts, heroisms, enemies
Who had to be crushed;
Causes that had to be fought for.
He had no time before the war
For bright skies, fields, the warm
Sun, his woman – only
Causes that had to be fought for.

I see him now after the war
In my lifetime. I notice his love
Of the sun, bright skies, fields, his woman:
Causes that have to be fought for.

Alan Bold

Let us be different

Let us be different,
Let us not be the same,
You will be you, I will be me,
Each of us has our own name.

You do things your way,
In the light you have found,
You must be true to what you know,
And stand on your own ground.

Until we can learn
To honour each other,
To hear and know what makes us real
We can't love one another.

But when that time comes,
Though many the flowers,
From different roots, we shall be shown
That one earth is ours.

Kathy Galloway

There will be peace between us

In laughter I will find you,
So many joys I will have shared with you,
They will become the measure of our time,
And there will be love between us
And there will be peace between us.

In tears I will find you,
So many times I will have cried for you,
I will offer you my song to ease your pain
And there will be love between us
And there will be peace between us.

In anger I will find you,
So many times I will have hated you,
But your tenderness will disarm me,
And there will be love between us
And there will be peace between us.

In losing I will find you,
So many times I will be without you,
But the things that you have given will not leave me,
And there will be love between us,
And there will be peace between us.

Kathy Galloway

Say 'no' to peace

Say 'no' to peace
if what they mean by peace
is the quiet misery of hunger,
the frozen stillness of fear,
the silence of broken spirits,
the unborn hopes of the oppressed.

Tell them that peace
is the shouting of children at play,
the babble of tongues set free,
the thunder of dancing feet,
and a father's voice singing.

Say 'no' to peace
if what they mean by peace
is a rampart of gleaming missiles,
the arming of distant wars,
money at ease in its castle
and grateful poor at the gate.

Tell them that peace
is the hauling down of flags,
the forging of guns into ploughs,
the giving of fields to the landless,
and hunger a fading dream.

Brian Wren

Thanksgiving

An Act of Thanksgiving

Minister

We offer to almighty God our thanksgiving for the many
blessings with which he has enriched our lives.

For The Queen and her family, and all who under her bear
the responsibility of government:
Thanks be to God.

For those who serve in the Armed Forces:
Thanks be to God.

For doctors, nurses, chaplains, and all who minister to those
in need or distress:
Thanks be to God.

For the unity of all people within the Commonwealth:
Thanks be to God.

For those whose sacrifices have contributed to our peace:
Thanks be to God.

For the Royal British Legion:
Thanks be to God.

The Promise of His Glory

Thanks for true peace

Risen Jesus,
we thank you for your greeting,
'Peace be with you.'
The shalom of God, deep lasting peace;
peace that brings inner calm;
that keeps a person steady in the storm;
that faces the persecutor without fear
and proclaims the good news with courage and with joy.

This is the peace that reconciles
sister to brother, black to white,
rich and poor, young and old;
but not a peace that is quiet
in the face of oppression and injustice.
This is peace with God,
the peace that passes understanding.
Amen.

John Johansen-Berg

A general thanksgiving

Almighty God, Father of all mercies,
we your unworthy servants
give you most humble and hearty thanks
for all your goodness and loving-kindness.
We bless you for our creation, preservation
and all the blessings of this life;
but above all for your immeasurable love
in the redemption of the world
by our Lord Jesus Christ,
for the means of grace, and for the hope of glory.
And give us, we pray,
such a sense of all your mercies,
that our hearts may be unfeignedly thankful,
and that we show forth your praise,
not only with our lips, but in our lives;
by giving up ourselves to your service,
and by walking before you
in holiness and righteousness, all our days;
through Jesus Christ our Lord,
to whom with you and the Holy Spirit,
be all honour and glory,
for ever and ever.
Amen.

Common Worship: The Daily Office

Intercessions

Minister
>   Let us pray to Almighty God for the needs of the world.

>   Where there is war and conflict, we pray for peace
>   and security;
>   where there is injustice and oppression, we pray for
>   justice and freedom;
>   where there is hatred and distrust, we pray for harmony
>   and understanding.
>   **Lord, in your mercy, hear our prayer.**

>   We pray for world leaders and all who exercise
>   influence over others,
>   that they may act wisely and justly and seek the
>   common good;
>   for the United Nations and all international organizations
>   working for justice and peace,
>   that they may be strengthened and upheld by your presence.
>   **Lord, in your mercy, hear our prayer.**

>   We pray for all who suffer as a result of war,
>   in body and mind or spirit;
>   for all who have lost their homes and possessions.
>   **Lord, in your mercy, hear our prayer.**

>   We pray for all who have died in war;
>   those who have taken up arms;
>   those caught up in conflicts in any way;
>   and all innocent victims of war and violence.
>   **Lord, in your mercy, hear our prayer.**

>   We offer these prayers through our Lord and Saviour
>   Jesus Christ.
>   **Merciful Father, accept these prayers**
>   **for the sake of your Son,**
>   **our Saviour, Jesus Christ. Amen.**

York Service, altered

Prayers for those who have suffered from war

Let us pray for all who suffer as a result of war:

for the injured and the disabled,
for the mentally distressed,
and for those whose faith in God and humanity
has been weakened and destroyed . . .

for the homeless and refugees,
for those who are hungry,
and for all who have lost their livelihood and security . . .

for those who mourn their dead,
those who have lost husband or wife,
children or parents,
and especially for those who have no hope in Christ
to sustain them in their grief . . .

Here follows a short silence.

Lord, in your mercy
hear our prayer.

Almighty God, our heavenly Father
infinite in wisdom, love and power:
have compassion on those for whom we pray;
and help us to use all suffering
in the cause of your kingdom;
through him who gave himself for us on the cross,
Jesus Christ your Son, our Lord.
Amen.

The Promise of His Glory

Prayers for peace

Let us pray for the peace of the world;
for statespeople and rulers, that they may have wisdom
to know and courage to do what is right . . .

for all who work to improve international relationships,
that they may find the true way to reconcile people
of different race, colour and creed . . .

and for men and women the world over, that they may
have justice and freedom, and live in security and peace . . .

Here follows a short silence.

Most gracious God and Father,
in whose will is our peace:
turn our hearts and the hearts of all to yourself,
that by the power of your Spirit
the peace which is founded on righteousness
may be established throughout the whole world;
through Jesus Christ our Lord.
Amen.

The Promise of His Glory

A prayer for unity, peace and justice
God of love and peace,
we pray for your Church throughout the world.
By your Holy Spirit,
draw your scattered people into visible unity,
and make your Church
a sign of hope to our divided world.

We pray for our country and Commonwealth.
Give wisdom and strength to The Queen,
govern those who make the laws,
guide those who direct our common life
and grant that together
we may seek the welfare of the whole people.

We pray for those in authority in every land.
Give them wisdom to know
and courage to do what is right.
Encourage all who work for peace,
who strive to improve international relations,
who seek new ways of reconciling
peoples to each other.

We pray for those who are homeless,
those who are refugees,
those who are hungry,
those who are oppressed.

Help us to live in peace,
to work for a world
where evil and poverty are banished
and human life reflects the radiance
of your kingdom.

Rejoicing in the communion of saints
we remember those whom you have gathered
from the storms of this world
into the peace of your presence
and give you thanks for those dear to us
whose memory we treasure.
Grant that we, at the last
may receive with them
the crown of life that never fades;
through Jesus Christ our Lord.
Amen.

Andrew Scobie

Show us the way to peace
Hiroshima,
Bosnia,
Belfast,
the names slip through our fingers
like bloodstained beads.

As we tell the story,
tell us,
tell us,
tell us,
the way
to peace.

Kosovo,
Nagasaki,
Nuremberg,
still they come, countless numbers:
People hounded, refugees tramping the road
out of hell, into hell.

Where will it stop?
Show us,
show us,
show us,
the way to peace.
Five for sorrow,
ten for joy,
May what has been sown in pain
be reaped in hope.
Amen.

Kate McIlhagga

Two prayers to follow the example of Jesus
Risen, reigning Christ,
in you past, present and future
are brought together in one great hope.
Renew our faith in you,
so that the past may not hinder us,
nor the present overwhelm us,
or the future frighten us.
You have brought us this far,
continue to lead us
until our hope is fulfilled
and we join with all God's people
in never-ending praise;
for your name's sake.
Amen.

*Prayer from the CTBI worship material
for The Queen's Golden Jubilee, 2002*

Father in heaven,
form in us the likeness of your Son
and deepen his life within us.
Send us as witnesses of gospel joy
into a world of fragile peace and broken promises.
Touch all hearts with your love
so we may, in turn, love each other.
Through Christ our Lord.
Amen.

*From St Benedict's Prayer Book:
concluding prayer for Saturday morning*

For our divided world
>Heavenly Father, whose heart is selfless love,
>take pity on our divided world;
>and grant that we may follow in the steps of your Son
>in giving ourselves to the service of others
>and reaching out to the marginalized and the despised,
>that peace and justice may triumph
>and your kingdom come on earth.
>In Christ's name we pray.
>**Amen.**

CTBI Group

A prayer to be a peacemaker
>Help me, O Lord, to make peace where I am,
>To turn dividing walls into bridges,
>And bring friendship in the place of strife,
>To be a neighbour to those near at hand
>And to those far away,
>Through Jesus Christ our Lord.
>**Amen.**

Prayers from the Orthodox Tradition

Prayers for peace from the liturgies of St John Chrysostom and St Basil

> In peace, let us pray to the Lord.
> **Lord, have mercy.**
>
> For the peace from above and the salvation of our souls, let us pray to the Lord.
> **Lord, have mercy.**
>
> For the peace of the whole world, for the welfare of the holy churches of God and the unity of all, let us pray to the Lord.
> **Lord, have mercy.**
>
> Let us pray to the Lord for an angel of peace, a faithful guide, guardian of souls and of our bodies.
> **Grant this prayer, O Lord.**
>
> Let us pray to the Lord for that which is good and useful to our souls, as well as the peace of the world.
> **Grant this prayer, O Lord.**
>
> Let us pray to the Lord for the completion of our lives in peace and repentance.
> **Grant this prayer, O Lord.**
>
> For a Christian end to our lives, peaceful, without shame and without suffering, and for a good account before the judgement seat of Christ, let us ask the Lord.
> **Grant this prayer, O Lord.**

Byzantine Church of Antioch

Anaphora of James, the brother of our Lord:
from the Divine Liturgy of St James

Account these our unworthy selves to be worthy of this
salvation, that freed from all guilt and united together by the
chain of love we may greet one another with the holy and
divine kiss of peace and that we may offer glory and thanks
to you and your only Son and to your Holy Spirit, all holy
and good, and adorable and life-giving, who is of one
substance with you, now and for ever, world without end.
Amen. Bless us, Lord.

Peace be with you all.
And with your spirit.

Syriac Church of Antioch

Chaldean Liturgy:
Offertory Song from the Mass of the Lord's Circumcision

May my peace be in you. Glory to God. Peace and safety
 earth; joy and hope to all humanity, without distinction.
Such is the good news of the birth and mission of Christ,
yesterday, today and for ever.

How beautiful are the steps of the messengers of the good
news of peace! Christ has called us to live in love, far from
dispute: neither to oppress, to be jealous, to humiliate, nor to
judge. He has called us to act with good will to wipe out all
discord. And the Lord will reward our efforts. Happy are the
peacemakers! That is the teaching of Jesus Christ. Peace
cannot reign without friendship, sincere dialogue.

Love, justice, truth and equality are the guarantees of lasting
peace. 'My peace I leave you, my peace I give to you.' O
Lord of peace, may we live in respect of each other, in a
spirit of truth and affirmation, rejecting all jealousy,
overcoming evil with patience, wiping it away with pardon
and bringing in (the reign of) peace through goodness.

Chaldean Church

Prayers for Understanding between People of Different Faiths

We include these prayers for those who may wish to pray in this way. We recognize that some member Churches of CTBI, while still desiring understanding between peoples, may not be happy to use these particular forms.

O God
From whom on different paths
All of us have come.
To whom on different paths
All of us are going.
Make strong in our hearts what unites us;
Build bridges across all that divides us.
United make us rejoice in our diversity
At one in our witness to that peace
Which you, O God, alone can give.
Amen.

> *The Soul of Europe Prayer – used by an organization working to reconcile war-torn communities in Bosnia from different faith backgrounds*

Eternal God, whose image lies in the hearts of all people,
we live among peoples whose ways are different from ours,
whose faiths are foreign to us,
whose tongues are unintelligible to us.
Help us to remember that you love all people with
your great love,
that all religion is an attempt to respond to you,
that the yearnings of other hearts are much like our own
and are known to you.
Help us to recognize you in the words of truth,
the things of beauty, the actions of love about us.
We pray through Christ, who is a stranger to no one
land more than another, and to every land no less than
to another.

> *Prayer from the World Council of Churches, Vancouver Assembly, 1983*

Remembrance

An Act of Remembrance

All stand.
A representative group may go to stand by the war memorial in
the church, or by the poppy wreath that was carried in at the
beginning of the service.

Minister
> Let us recall before God
> those who have given their lives in the cause of freedom
> and in the service of others,
> especially those known to us.

The list of those to be remembered by name may be read.
Representatives of The Royal British Legion or other appointed
people shall say:

> They shall grow not old as we that are left grow old:
> Age shall not weary them, nor the years condemn.
> At the going down of the sun and in the morning
> We will remember them.
> **We will remember them.**

The Last Post is sounded.

Silence is kept for two minutes.

Reveille is sounded.

Minister
> There is music in the midst of desolation
> **And a glory that shines upon our tears.**

or

> We will remember them.
> **We will remember them.**

Minister

Almighty and eternal God,
from whose love in Christ we cannot be parted,
either by death or life:
hear our prayers and thanksgivings
for all whom we remember this day;
fulfil in them the purpose of your love;
and bring us all, with them, to your eternal joy;
through Jesus Christ our Lord.
Amen.

York Service

For Armistice Day

Remember what you will.
Remember the sacrifice, the blood, the death,
The loyalties forged, the times shared, the glory –
Remember what you will.

Remember what you will;
The ideals, rights, justifications,
The tyranny, the bravery, the hope,
The trust betrayed, consciences crushed, innocence lost;
Remember what you will.

Remember what you will.
Remember the youth destroyed, faces saved.
Remember the scars, the wounded minds and bodies,
Families destroyed or uncreated,
The waste, the gains.
And all things avoided or lost;
Bloodbath,
Sacrifice
Or bloodletting –
Remember what you will.

Remember what you will.
Remember what you will –
But *remember.*

James Murdoch Ewing

Remembering at the war memorial

They went to meet Charlotte, who was standing to one side with
a bunch of rosemary in her hand. From where she stood Charlotte
could see the river and the bridge where she and John Malcolm
had said goodbye those years ago. She was glad her last image of
him was his handsome happy face smiling at her. It was something
that she could keep inside her to help her through the years
ahead. She was glad too that John Malcolm's name was carved on
the town's war memorial. Having his name there meant that there
was somewhere to visit and lay flowers, a place to remember . . .
to remember every one of them . . . Annie's two boys, Rory and
Ewan, Helen's young man, the gardener's lad, the stable boy, the
fifteen men and boys from the village who had joined up on the
same day and died together, Eddie Kane and all the others.

Charlotte raised her head when the minister began to read out the
list of names. As he reached the name of John Malcolm Dundas,
without letting go of Francis's arm, Maggie reached out and took
Charlotte's hand.

Theresa Breslin

A prayer in remembrance

In remembrance of those –
throughout time, all over the world –
who have died in war,
we pray urgently today
that children, women and men
may become makers of peace.

We pray for children growing up
in violent surroundings
or thinking, talking and playing in warlike ways.
God, give to our people a new challenge,
new ways in which to test their strength
in sharing power and risking non-violence.

We pray for women who are silent
while their male partners engage
in any part of the business of war.
God, give to your people a new courage
to question accepted dogma,
and dream about the things that make for peace.

We pray for men brought up to believe
that might is manly – and for men who think otherwise
and so are labelled cowardly or weak.
God, give to your people a new determination
to struggle for justice and peace
instead of for 'extra shares' and superiority.

O God, we pray for –
new awareness of the battlefield within us
new ways of challenging aggressive instincts
new thought-patterns, language and ideas
new appreciation of the world as one community
new methods of dialogue and negotiation
new attempts to befriend those different from ourselves
new readiness to forgive and reconcile,
new visions, new love, new hope . . .
and a new faith that the peace that passes understanding
can reach out from within us to embrace the world.

Kate Compston

Litany of remembrance
In the rising of the sun
and its going down,
we remember them.

In the blowing of the wind
and in the chill of winter,
we remember them.

In the blueness of the sky
and in the warmth of summer,
we remember them.

In the rustling of leaves
and in the beauty of autumn,
we remember them.

When we are lost
and sick at heart,
we remember them.

When we have joys
we yearn to share,
we remember them.

So long as we live,
they too shall live,
for we remember them.

St Paul's Cathedral, Los Angeles

It cannot

Death
does not hold me,
though it touches
as I pass by.

It cannot deafen
your whisper of love,
though it sometimes
fills my ears.

It cannot blind me
to the lights of hope,
though its darkness
can make me for
a moment grope.

It cannot freeze my feeling
or cool your spirit's warmth;
for its heat is transitory,
its pain is a passing sore.

It cannot drain my soul
of all the memories of
smile and tear,
though it clamours to
empty my living.

Death,
truly you are
a mask
and I can,
and do
deny your power.

Donald Macaskill

Pledging and Commitment

Minister
Let us pledge ourselves anew to the service of God and all humanity.

Silence is kept

Before God
we pledge ourselves
to establish justice and peace,
to feed the hungry and heal the broken
to welcome the refugee and the stranger
to console the bereaved,
to bring hope to those in want
so that all may rejoice
in the glorious liberty of the children of God
Amen.

or

Minister
In silence let us prepare ourselves to make our commitment.
A brief silence follows, and then

As Jesus taught us we commit ourselves
to welcome strangers into our midst,
to care for the poor,
to love our neighbours as ourselves
and to establish justice in our community.
In the name of God
and in the power of the Holy Spirit
we pledge ourselves to work for peace:
peace in our homes,
peace in our communities,
peace in the world.
Amen.

Affirmations of Faith

We believe God made this world,
God loves this world, God lives in this world.
We believe God holds it and cradles it in loving hands:
holding its pain,
caring for every memory
of every person in conflict.
We believe God loves each human being,
on every side of every struggle,
who has given of themselves,
even to death,
for their friends and family and country.
We believe violence breaks God's heart;
bullets tear through God's realm;
and war opposes God's love.
But we believe love lives longer than hatred;
hope burns away at despair;
God calls to us from the violence,
and we can work in love for a better world.
So be it.

Seasons of the Spirit

We express our trust in Jesus
We believe in Jesus Christ,
crucified, risen and ascended,
who has battled with evil and won.
He has won with the power of his love,
love which is stronger than all the evil
and violence in the world.
We believe in the power of his love,
power alive in his people today,
power to overcome fear and suspicion.
And we put our trust in his love alone
and we turn away from all weapons
that kill our innocent brothers and sisters.
For we cannot rely on the weapons of this world
when all our security, hope and life is in Jesus.

We believe in the power of the risen Christ,
for only he can give us inner security.
And we turn away from the evil of mass destruction,
of arming ourselves while others starve,
of trusting the weapons of evil
to safeguard the true and the good.
We believe in Jesus Christ:
and we trust his power of love and nothing else.

BCC Mannafest, Lincoln Cathedral, 1981

An affirmation of faith written by two 14-year-old boys
We believe in God,
who made the sun and the sky, the stars and the sea,
who calls us to live responsibly.

We believe in Jesus Christ
who became human
who healed the sick
who talked to children
who made friends with sinners.
He burned brightly and offended many.
His journey was one of life and death and resurrection.
His light continues to shine in darkness.

We believe in the Holy Spirit
who inspires the scriptures
and whose breath we breathe.

We believe that God calls us to be a community
committed to one another
offering a welcome to everyone
old and young
rich and poor
strong and weak.

We believe that God calls us to be
peacemakers
workers for justice
brothers and sisters
a light for our world.
Amen.

The Iona Community

Affirmation
>We believe in God,
>
>God the Holy One,
>God the Maker,
>God who woke the clays of a cold earth to life,
>God who glories in men and women,
>children of his love.
>
>We debased his holy will
>and sowed the seeds of pain and death.
>
>Yet in his steadfast love God pitied us;
>he came to us in Jesus Christ,
>his own dear Son,
>our joy and gladness.
>
>Seed, though dead and fallen,
>burst to life and rose again,
>our resurrection.
>
>God breathes eternity into our souls,
>and makes us flames of heaven's fire,
>for the healing of the nations.
>
>And so we bless and glorify his holy name.
>In life, in death,
>beyond life, beyond death,
>God is with us.
>
>Thanks be to God.

Fleur Houston

Assurance
>The desert will sing and rejoice
>**and the wilderness blossom with flowers.**
>
>All will see the Lord's splendour,
>**see the Lord's greatness and power.**
>
>Tell everyone who is anxious:
>**Be strong and don't be afraid.**

The blind will be able to see;
the deaf will be able to hear.

The lame will leap and dance;
those who can't speak will shout.

They will hammer their swords into ploughs
and their spears into pruning-knives;

the nations will live in peace;
they will train for war no more.

This is the promise of God;
God's promise will be fulfilled.
Iona Abbey Worship Book: Isaiah 35; Micah 4.1-4

**We look forward with hope
to new possibilities and new vision.
We trust in God who brings life out of death
and who calls us to love our enemies,
and seek the peace which he alone can give.
Amen.**
CTBI Group

Endings and Blessings

Endings

> **Lord Jesus Christ,**
> **Son of the living God,**
> **teach us to live in the ways of peace and justice,**
> **to wage peace rather than war;**
> **so that we may come**
> **by the power of the Holy Spirit**
> **as one family to the kingdom of the Father**
> **where you live for ever and ever.**
> **Amen.**

Minister

> Grant, Lord, that we may live in your fear,
> die in your favour,
> rest in your peace,
> rise in your power,
> and reign in your glory.

> The grace of our Lord Jesus Christ,
> The love of God and the fellowship of the Holy Spirit
> Be with us all now and for ever more.
> **Amen.**

> May the peace of God
> which is beyond all understanding
> keep your hearts and minds in the knowledge and love of
> God
> and of his Son, Jesus Christ.
> **Amen.**

Blessings

Minister

> May the Lord bless you and keep you.
> May his face shine upon you and be gracious to you.
> May he look upon you with kindness and give you his peace.
> **Amen.**

Minister

God grant to the living grace,
to the departed rest,
to the Church, the Queen, the Commonwealth
and to all people, peace and concord,
and to us and all his servants life everlasting,
and the blessing of God almighty,
Father, Son and Holy Spirit be with you all evermore
Amen.

Go in the strength of God's Spirit
lighting the lamps of justice and peace
with the oil of righteousness;
and the blessing of God almighty
The Father, the Son and the Holy Spirit
Be among you and remain with you always.
Amen.

The God of peace fill you with all joy and hope in believing;
and the blessing of God almighty, the Father, the Son and the
Holy Spirit,
be among you.
Amen.

The God of peace, who brought again from the dead our
Lord Jesus Christ, that great shepherd of the sheep, make you
perfect in every good work to do his will; and the blessing of
God almighty, the Father, the Son and the Holy Spirit, be
among you and remain with you always.
Amen.

The peace of God, which passes all understanding, keep
your hearts and minds in the knowledge and love of God
and of his Son Jesus Christ our Lord; and the blessing of God
almighty, the Father, the Son and the Holy Spirit, be among
you, and remain with you always.
Amen.

Hymns and Music

Suggestions for hymns

Opening hymns

- Christ, whose glory fills the skies
- Christ is made the sure foundation
- Eternal Ruler of the ceaseless round
- Immortal, invisible, God only wise
- All people that on earth do dwell
- Praise to the Holiest in the height
- Praise to the Lord, the Almighty, the King of creation.

Wesley's 'Christ, whose glory fills the skies' was recited each day as a prayer by Bishop Wilson, while he was imprisoned and tortured in Changi prison in 1943.

As alternatives to responsorial psalms

- The Lord's my Shepherd (23)
- The King of love my shepherd is (23)
- O God, you are my God, for you my soul is athirst (63)
- Send forth your spirit, O Lord, and renew the face of the earth (104)
- I will bless your name for ever, my God and my King (145).

Before the Gospel

- Blest are the pure in heart
- O Lord, all the world belongs to you
- Praise to God, whose word was spoken
- Behold, the mountain of the Lord
- Praise to the Holiest in the height.

After the Act of Remembrance

- Christ be our light
- Be thou my vision
- O God, our help in ages past
- Thy kingdom come, O God, Thy rule, O Christ, begin
- Make me a channel of your peace
- In Christ there is no east or west
- *For the Navy*: Eternal Father, strong to save
- *The Aviator's Hymn*: Lord of the universe and space (Tune: Melita).

Concluding hymn after Act of Commitment

- Lord, for the years your love has kept and guided
- We shall go out with hope of resurrection
- Christ is the King! O friends rejoice
- Thine be the glory, risen, conquering Son
- Let there be peace on earth, and let it begin with me
- Forth in the peace of Christ we go
- Guide me, O thou great Redeemer.

New hymns and music for Remembrance

What shall we pray?
In Scotland Remembrance Sunday, when the nation honours those who have died in war, can be a fraught occasion. It brings back unspeakably painful memories to some; offends others; and puzzles young people who have seen only pictures of war. In this song, representatives of a local congregation identified the different people who would be reacting to services of remembrance, holding them together before God with the same prayer.

What shall we pray?

John L. Bell

1. What shall we pray for those__ who died,
those on whose death__ our lives re - lied?__
Si - lenced by war but not de - nied,__
God give them peace.   peace that lasts.__

What shall we pray for those who died,
those on whose death our lives relied?
Silenced by war but not denied.
God give them peace.

What shall we pray for those who mourn
friendships and love, their fruit unborn?
Though years have passed, hearts still are torn:
God give them peace.

What shall we pray for those who live
tied to the past they can't forgive,
haunted by terrors they relive?
God give them peace.

What shall we pray for those who know
nothing of war, and cannot show
grief or regret for friend or foe?
God give them peace.

What shall we pray for those who fear
war, in some guise, may reappear
looking attractive and sincere?
God give them peace.

God give us peace and, more than this,
show us the path where justice is;
and let us never be remiss
working for peace that lasts.

Carnwadric Parish Church Worship Group and John L. Bell

Forgive us, Lord, our lamps are faint

Gerry Fitzpatrick

The Lord's Prayer

Gerry Fitzpatrick

You raise the dead

Words: the Roman Missal;
Music: Martin Morran, © Kevin Mayhew

How blest are those who have died

Words and music © Noel S Donnelly

How blest are those who have died in the Lord! Let them rest from their la-bours, let them rest_____ for their good works go with them, for their good works go with them. E -

ter-nal rest give un-to_them, Oh Lord, and let per-pet-ual

light shine on them! May they rest in peace!
(choir doubles organ)

May they rest in peace! peace!

Psalm 129

Words and music © Noel S Donnelly

Come to me and I shall give you rest.

From the depths I call to you,
Love and mer - cy flow from you,
In the dark I hope for you,
Weak and frail we come to you,

lis - ten, Lord, and hear my plead - ing.
Lord of life and kind Re - deem - er.
you are light of new day dawn - ing.
God of love and new be - gin - ning.

Blessed are the Peacemakers

A service of reflection and reconciliation

Gathering

The Ministers enter and take their places.
Standards and pennants may be brought in and presented.

Minister
Grace to you and peace from God our Father and the Lord
Jesus Christ.
Thanks be to God.

We have come together to worship God and to remember
those who have lived and died in war as they sought to serve
others. We will confess with shame those occasions when
nations have lightly chosen war rather than peace. We will
pray for all who still suffer as a result of war and we will
commit ourselves to serve their needs and to work with all
our strength to see peace and justice established throughout
the world.

The Beatitudes
*Three lamps or candles are brought in by children and young
people and put in a prominent place. While this is being
done the Beatitudes may be said or sung by a Minister and
the people.*

Blessed are the poor in spirit,
for theirs is the kingdom of heaven.

Blessed are those who mourn,
for they shall be comforted.

Blessed are the gentle,
for they shall inherit the earth.

Blessed are those who hunger and thirst for what is right,
for they shall be satisfied.

Blessed are the merciful,
for mercy shall be shown to them.

Blessed are the pure in heart,
for they shall see God.

Blessed are the peacemakers,
for they shall be called children of God.

Blessed are those who are persecuted in the cause of right,
for theirs is the kingdom of heaven.

Blessed are you when others revile you and persecute you,
and utter all kinds of evil against you falsely for my sake.

Rejoice and be glad,
for your reward is in heaven.

Minister
Grace to you and peace from God the Father and the Lord
Jesus Christ.
Thanks be to God.

A hymn is sung.

Declaration of the mercy of God

Minister
You raise the dead to life in the Spirit:
Lord, have mercy.
Lord, have mercy.

You bring pardon and peace to the sinner:
Christ, have mercy.
Christ, have mercy.

You bring light to those in darkness:
Lord, have mercy.
Lord, have mercy.

Collect

Ever-living God,
rejoicing in the example of those who have gone before us,
we pray that, like them, we may strive for justice and peace
and work together for the coming of your kingdom
in the name of Jesus Christ, our Saviour.
Amen.

or

God our Father,
you reveal that those who work for peace
will be called your children.
Help us to work without ceasing
for that justice
which brings true and lasting peace.
We ask this through our Lord Jesus Christ, your Son,
who lives and reigns with you and the Holy Spirit,
one God, for ever and ever.
Amen.

Proclaiming and receiving the Word

*The readings may be taken from the lectionary of the Sunday,
or any of the special lessons set out below may be used.*

Old Testament reading

Amos 5.14-15,21-24
Isaiah 2.2-5
Micah 4.1-5

*A psalm may be said or sung in any way appropriate to the
occasion.*

New Testament reading

Romans 8.18-25
1 Corinthians 1.18-31
2 Corinthian 5.16-end

A hymn is sung.

Gospel

St Matthew 5.1-12
St Matthew 5.43-end
St John 13.31-35

Sermon

*Stories, poems or reflections may be read in addition
to or in the place of the sermon or one of the readings.
A testimony may be given.*

*An Affirmation or Declaration of Faith may be used.
See pp. 41–44.*

Remembering

Sorrow for the wrongs of the past

*All stand. The three readers go to stand by the candles or lamps
that were carried in. One is extinguished after each voice has
spoken, and all three are relit after the absolution.*

Minister
Jesus said: I give you a new commandment, that you should love
one another as I have loved you.

Voice 1
> For not being prepared for peace;
> for not being prepared for a new way of living;
> for not being prepared for the arrival of love's realm;
> *[Extinguish lamp or candle]*
> **Forgive us; our lamps are faint.**

Voice 2
> For not being ready for God's work on earth;
> for not being ready to speak out when love calls;
> for not being ready to stand firm in the Gospel;
> *[Extinguish lamp or candle.]*
> **Forgive us; our lamps are fading.**

Voice 3

> For not making plans to destroy armaments;
> for not making plans to wipe out injustice;
> for not making plans to love our enemy;
> *[Extinguish lamp or candle.]*
> **Forgive us; our light is running out.**

Absolution

Minister

> May almighty God have mercy upon you,
> pardon and deliver you from all your sins,
> fill your souls with the possibility of heaven
> and strengthen you with the oil of righteousness,
> through Jesus Christ our Lord.
> **Amen.**

Minister

Let us now remember those whose lives have been sacrificed
to build a world of justice and peace.

Silence is kept for two minutes.

Minister

> Light up the world
> with the new hope you have been given;
> Make ready the world for the coming of Christ.
> **Amen.**

At this point the lamps or candles are relit one by one.
                                    Seasons of the Spirit

A hymn may be sung.

Praying – thanksgiving and interceding

Thanksgiving

Let us give thanks for the loving kindness of God
and his strength given in every time of need.

We bless you, O God, for the courage, devotion to duty
and self-sacrifice of those who in past conflicts
gave themselves that we may live in peace.
We bless you for the witness of those
who today make sacrifices, which challenge us to
    search for peace.
We bless you for those who invite us to share their
    vision of a new world
in which your creation is cherished and
every human life valued,
for Jesus' sake.
Amen.

Interceding

Petitions should be offered for:
- *the unity of God's Church throughout the world;*
- *the people of our islands;*
- *The Queen, and all in government;*
- *the countries of the Commonwealth and other nations of our world;*
- *those who work for peace, seeking to overcome hatred between the nations;*
- *those who in the service of their country are called to be peacemakers where there is conflict;*
- *refugees, the hungry, the homeless, the stranger, the oppressed.*

Or there may be free prayer in which people intercede for peace and justice in their own words; or prayers from the Intercessions section may be used (see pp.26–31).

Minister
We say together the prayer that Jesus gave us,
trusting that God's kingdom of peace and justice will come.

> **Our Father in heaven,**
> **hallowed be your name.**
> **Your kingdom come,**
> **your will be done**
> **on earth as in heaven.**
> **Give us today our daily bread.**
> **Forgive us our sins**
> **as we forgive those who sin against us.**
> **Save us from the time of trial,**
> **and deliver us from evil.**
> **For the kingdom, the power and the glory are yours**
> **now and for ever. Amen.**

Pledging

Minister
In silence let us prepare ourselves to make our commitment.

A brief silence follows, and then:

> **As Jesus taught us, we commit ourselves**
> **to welcome strangers into our midst,**
> **to care for the poor,**
> **to love our neighbours as ourselves**
> **and to establish justice in our community.**
> **In the name of God**
> **and in the power of the Holy Spirit**
> **we pledge ourselves to work for peace:**
> **peace in our homes,**
> **peace in our communities,**
> **peace in the world.**
> **Amen.**

A hymn may be sung.

Sending out

Minister

> Go forth into the world as pilgrims of God,
> upheld by the hands of him who created you.
> Go forth to discover new life in Christ,
> Son of the living God, who died for you.
> Go in the strength and joy of God's Spirit,
> whose indwelling power will renew you.
> Go in the name of the Holy Trinity
> to light the lamps of justice and peace
> with the oil of righteousness.
>
> *Seasons of the Spirit (altered)*

The National Anthem may be sung now or after the blessing.

The Blessing

> The God of peace fill you with all joy and hope in believing;
> and the blessing of God almighty, the Father, the Son
> and the Holy Spirit,
> be among you and remain with you always.
> **Amen.**

The National Anthem is sung at this point if it was not sung before the blessing.

The standards and pennants are returned to their bearers and led out by the bearers of the candles or lamps.

A hymn may be sung.

Commemorating National or Local Tragedy or Remembrance

Prayers, readings and worship resources

Introduction

In 1966 the whole of the United Kingdom was shaken by the tragedy that occurred in Aberfan in Wales when a waste tip slid down a mountainside into the mining village, killing many children in Pantglas Junior School.

In recent years there have been a series of occasions of national and local tragedy, which have stirred the feelings and emotions of many people. Examples of this are the death of Princess Diana, the Dunblane tragedy, the murders of two children in Soham and the 11 September attacks in America. The Presidents of CTBI have asked that some advice and suggestions to be used on future similar occasions should be provided in this book.

Many people in these islands have either infrequent contact with the Church or no contact at all. As the rituals of the Church have ceased to nourish many people, new ways of dealing with tragedy have arisen. These include the laying of flowers; the tying of flowers to railings, lamp posts, trees or seats; the tying of scarves to football posts; and the lighting of candles on pavements. At the same time, many people unfamiliar with the Church have turned to the churches for a welcome and help on such occasions and have sought to bring their own symbols with them.

We would suggest that the following pointers may be helpful in times of local or national tragedy.
- Make every effort to keep cathedrals, churches and other places of worship open and to give free access.
- Have people on hand who will be available if necessary but who will not intrude.
- Make provision for people to lay flowers or light candles.
- Have a book of condolence for people to sign.
- Have available small cards containing words of comfort available, to give to them.
- Have prayers available on paper, for any who wish to take and use these in silence.
- Share the responsibility with Ministers of other Churches.
- A simple act of worship may be held – possibly every hour on the hour.

- Be aware that for some time people are not ready to hear of hope – just be with them in their pain.
- Be ready, when appropriate, to assure people of God's love and presence with them in their pain.
- Be aware that people of other faiths may come to join in the prayers; make them welcome.
- When people come to church services, adapt these to their needs and help them to feel welcome and at home.
- When people are ready, be prepared to move on and speak of good news and the Christian hope.
- At memorial services a year or more later, help people to look back but also to look forward.

Readings and Sayings

Readings that may be helpful

- Psalm 16: 'Preserve me O God, for in you I have taken refuge'
- Psalm 23: 'The Lord is my shepherd'
- Psalm 46.1-7: 'God is our refuge and strength'
- Psalm 84.1-7: 'How lovely is your dwelling-place'
- Isaiah 40.28-31: 'God will renew our strength'
- Isaiah 43.1b-2a: 'I will be with you'
- Isaiah 61.1-3: 'To comfort all who mourn'
- Lamentations 3.22-25: 'The steadfast love of the Lord never ceases'
- John 11.23-27: 'Your brother will rise again'
- John 14.1-6: 'Do not let your hearts be troubled'
- Romans 8.35-39: 'Nothing can separate us from the love of God'
- 1 Thessalonians 4.13-18: 'So we shall always be with the Lord'
- Revelation 21.1-7: 'He will wipe away every tear from their eye.'

Short sayings from the Bible

These may perhaps be distributed on small cards with a picture, or on photocopied sheets.

God is our refuge and strength,
a very present help in trouble.

Psalm 46.1

The steadfast love of the Lord never ceases.

Lamentations 3.22a

When you pass through the waters, I will be with you.

Isaiah 43.2a

I am the resurrection and the life.

John 11.25

Blessed are those who mourn,
for they shall be comforted.

Matthew 5.4

Sayings from other writers

From him we come. In him we are enfolded. To him
we return.

Julian of Norwich

Everything has being through the love of God.

Julian of Norwich

He did not say you will not be storm tossed, but he did
say you will not be overcome.

Julian of Norwich

But in all this I saw truly that we are not dead in the sight
of God nor does he ever depart from us; but he will never
have his full joy with us until we have our full joy in him,
truly seeing his fair, blessed face.

Julian of Norwich

All shall be well and all manner of things shall be well.

Julian of Norwich

Blessed be Jesus who is always near in times of stress.
Even when we cannot feel his presence he is close.

Margery Kempe

For those with faith, death is not extinguishing the light
but putting out the lamp because the dawn has come.

Rabindranath Tagore

Prayers

Prayers after a disaster

Gracious God,
through your Son you have taught us
that nothing in life or in death
is able to separate us from your love.
Look in mercy on all to whom great sorrow has come
through the *A* . . . in *X* . . .
Help those who are injured,
support those who are dying.
Strengthen the members of the emergency services
[*The appropriate services may be mentioned*]
and all who bring relief and comfort.
Console and protect
those who have lost loved ones.
Give your light in darkness
to all who are near to despair,
and assure them that you hold all souls in life;
through Jesus Christ our risen Lord.
Amen.

Derek Browning

Lord God,
fear comes in many guises into our lives.
It is legion:
the fear of the unknown
which blights our vision;
the fear of pain
which narrows our world;
the fear of failure
which challenges our confidence.

In this time of tragedy,
in this time of anger,
in this time of grief,
in this time of doubt,
come to us as the Father who stands alongside,
as the Son who brings hope,
as the Spirit Who brings healing.

We pray for all afflicted by the tragedy in . . . ;
we pray for those who have lost loved ones;
we pray for those who wait and wonder;
we pray for those whose lives have emptied.
We pray for those in pain, waiting for rescue,
and for those who lie in pain in hospital or at home.

We pray for those who bring help
through the emergency services,
through the diplomatic community
and through the acts of kindliness and neighbourliness
which bring a little ease and comfort.

We pray for those who think evil actions are justifiable
and those whose hearts and minds
are hard against humanity.
Stop them when we cannot;
Forgive them when we cannot.
Transform them when we cannot.

Prepare us for the world ahead
to work for peace, to strive for justice,
to change our ways
and to receive the gifts of grace and courage and faith.
For Christ's sake. **Amen.**

Panel on Worship, Church of Scotland

A prayer for those who suffer

God of unending mercy,
we pray with those who cry:
For women and men who are battered in body or spirit,
for children who sleep the fitful sleep of grief,
for all who are imprisoned by walls or worries,
for all who wonder if they can ever live again,
for the least, the lost and the last, and for the dead.

Christ, have mercy on those who cry;
Christ, have mercy on us when we turn away
    from the cries of others.
Give us the strength of compassion,
that we may never shield our eyes and hearts from pain,
but seek to heal and bless.

Bless us with courage and arm us with hope,
that we may lessen the suffering of our world.

Hear this our common prayer
and those of our hearts which we offer now.

Paul Sheppy

A prayer for a schoolfriend who has been killed

Loving God,
Jesus watched his friends in the streets.
They played at weddings and funerals,
but today it isn't a game for us;
we are sad and crying.
Help us to know that *N* is safe with you,
and when we remember *her*
help us to remember happy days
and laughter too.

Paul Sheppy

A prayer for a murder victim

O God,
we are angry,
we have been robbed of *N*
and *she* has been robbed of life.
We have wept
till there were no tears left to shed;
and still we weep.
We have shouted,
we have called to you.
Yet our voice returns empty
and the heavens seem deaf to our cry.
Your Son was murdered too.
O God,
we are weeping with you.

Paul Sheppy

A prayer for the victim of an accident

O God,
why *N*?
We want an answer,
but no answer is good enough;
for we really want *N*.
But *she* is gone,
and we are left with questions.
Grant us courage to leave *her* with you.
O God,
we want to believe.
Help us where faith runs out.

Paul Sheppy

For those who mourn

O God our refuge and our strength,
A very present help in trouble,
We seek your comfort and your blessing
For those who mourn the death of those they love,
For all whose lives are torn apart by violence,
For all the suffering people of the world;
Through Jesus Christ our Lord.

For the dead and for those who mourn

God of mercy, Lord of life,
you have made us in your image
to reflect your truth and light:
we give you thanks for *N*
and for the grace and mercy *he/she* received from you,
for all that was good in *his/her* life,
for the memories we treasure today.
(*Especially we thank you . . .*)

Silence

(Lord, in your mercy
hear our prayer.)

You promised eternal life to those who believe.
Remember for good this your servant *N*
as we also remember *him/her.*

Bring all who rest in Christ
into the fullness of your kingdom,
where sins have been forgiven
and death is no more.

Silence

(Lord, in your mercy
hear our prayer.)

Your mighty power brings joy out of grief
and life out of death.
Look in mercy on (. . . *and*) all who mourn.
Give them patient faith in times of darkness.
Strengthen them with the knowledge of your love.

Silence

(Lord, in your mercy
hear our prayer.)

You are tender towards your children
and your mercy is over all your works.
Heal the memories of hurt and failure.
Give us the wisdom and grace to use aright
the time that is left to us here on earth,
to turn to Christ and follow in his steps
in the way that leads to everlasting life.

Silence

(Lord, in your mercy
hear our prayer.)

God of mercy,
entrusting into your hands all that you have made
and rejoicing in your communion with all your
faithful people,
we make our prayers through Jesus Christ our Saviour.
Amen.

Common Worship: Pastoral Provision

Readings and Prayers
of Lamentation and Grief

Giving people the chance to express their feelings

I am weary with my moaning;
Every night I flood my bed with tears;
I drench my couch with my weeping.
My eye wastes away because of grief,
It grows weak because of all my foes.

Psalm 6.6-7

Thus says the Lord:
A voice in Ramah,
Weeping and great mourning,
Rachel weeping for her children
And refusing to be comforted
Because they are no more.

Jeremiah 31.15

Loving God
We are lost and it is dark;
We are hurt, but we feel nothing;
We know but we cannot take it in.
Be a light to our footsteps,
A balm to our wounds,
And lead us to your truth;
Through Jesus Christ
Your dead but risen Son.
Amen.

Derek Browning

Lord, there are times when I am worn out with grief,
With no way forward and no way back.
Surely you are supposed to hear my cries,
And have mercy and save me.
But still my pillow becomes wet from my tears;
My body loses its appetite;
My mind falters;
My soul is weak to the point of exhaustion.
As trouble overwhelms me,
And panic sets in and I have nowhere to turn,
My only words are to you;
God give me strength.
Amen.

Derek Browning

Lord,
Why me? Why this? Why now?
I see the bad times coming – I pray.
The bad times come – I pray.
The bad times get worse – I pray;
And what feels like nothing happens.
Where are you, God, when I need you?
Is it something I have said, is it something I have done?
What do I have to say, what do I have to do
So that I can hear your voice and know
    that you are with me?
Day and night – and nothing!

If only I knew the secret formula of words and actions
That unlocks your heart and prompts you to act.

Lord,
There are times when prayer is hard work,
And times when I wonder why I persevere with it.
My own needs empty my resources for living.
The needs of others drain my treasury of life.
I am left, emptied and drained, and I don't know what to do.
The lights go out, one by one, and darkness
    is my only companion.
Yet still I pray,
Sometimes beyond reason, sometimes beyond hope,
Asking again and again,

Laying bare my soul,
And stretching out my hands,
And believing even in this darkness
that you will hear and you will come.
Come, Lord, come!
            Derek Browning; Church of Scotland Panel on Worship

In the Jewish Tradition, psalms of lament and imprecation enabled people to rail against God and in some way to hold on to their faith. People who have suffered greatly or unexpectedly must feel free to express their anger against God as does this modern psalm, which begins by cursing God and ends with a muted expression of faith.

Psalm of grief

God I will curse you, for you are my enemy,
And my heart recoils from your touch.
Your loving kindness is a lie,
And your dealings are without mercy;
For I have seen the dying of my friend,
And I have witnessed the work of your hands upon her.

Daily you broke her body on the rack,
You exposed her skin to be scorched,
And into her belly you have thrust your knives.
You delivered her into the care of fools,
And those who were to heal her, handled her brutally.

In her desolation she prayed to be released,
But you turned your face from her plea.
At the sight of her agony you hardened your heart,
And carried her back from the grave.
You bestowed on her the pain of survival,
You caused her children to hope.

You laid your hand on her a second time,
You crushed her so that she could no more breathe.
You shrivelled up her bones with your fire,
She was dried out like a garment before the wind;
You consumed her flesh while she was yet alive.

How then shall I praise your compassion,
And how can I with integrity bless my God?

For like one who inflicts torture
Beyond what her victim can bear,
So untenderly did you give her to death;
And as one who can no longer wrestle for life,
Did she find peace within your arms.

Janet Morley

Expressions of Faith and Forgiveness

On other occasions, people who have experienced enormous tragedy show a tremendous faith. An example of such a person was the Baptist Minister in Aberfan.

The Revd Kenneth Hayes

Kenneth Hayes, Baptist Minister: born Risca, Glamorganshire, 1930; married with one son, and one son deceased; died Sheffield, 25 December 1997.

On 21 October 1966, in the mining village of Aberfan in South Wales, a colliery waste tip slid down a mountain and engulfed the village school, killing 144 people, 116 of them children. Those who saw the deeply moving *Timewatch* on the disaster, screened in October 1996, will recall two unforgettable images of Kenneth Hayes. One is the newsreel film of the 36-year-old minister of Zion English Baptist Church, whose own son Dyfrig was missing. He decided that his role was not to dig for bodies but to do what he could for souls. He helped methodically with the grisly task of establishing the death roll – in those first few days it was believed to be even higher than it actually was. On the Sunday after the disaster, the day after his son's body had been found, he preached in his chapel to an audience of journalists, many of them in tears throughout. In the awful months that followed, he and his wife kept the community afloat. They ran an appeal for toys for the surviving children of Aberfan that generated a huge and emotional response, as did the main disaster appeal. Kenneth Hayes's manse became the office in which the local solicitor took the statements that would confirm the Coal Board's culpability for the disaster.

The other unforgettable image was of Kenneth Hayes thirty years on, talking to the film makers with unnerving conviction:

> The end of chapter 8 of Romans is a great summary of faith –
> *What can separate us from the love of God* – it's a passage
> I always use when there's a personal tragedy or disaster and
> that's a message we always try to emphasise – *I am certain
> that nothing can separate us from the love of God, neither
> death nor life, neither angels or other heavenly rulers or
> powers, neither the present nor the future . . .*

As far as we're concerned now, we've still got two boys. We're only separated for a time. One day we're going to meet. The parting and the loneliness and being without him is terrible, but it's not for ever.

Only such unshakeable faith can have carried him through thirty years of trauma. When he officiated at Aberfan Cemetery on the anniversary of the disaster in October 1997, he did so with a firm strength that belied his very frail frame.

Iain McLean

Others have shown a remarkable readiness to forgive.

On Sunday 8 November 1987, as people gathered around the Enniskillen cenotaph, an IRA bomb exploded. Eleven people died; there was extensive damage. Gordon Wilson and his daughter Marie were buried in the rubble. As they held hands, Marie, a nurse, died. That same evening Gordon Wilson gave a spontaneous and memorable interview to a BBC reporter. Some criticized him for what he said; others were amazed at the spirit of reconciliation he expressed. Later he wrote:

> I like to think that it was the real Gordon Wilson who spoke to the BBC's reporter, Mike Gaston, on the evening of the bomb, when I said, 'I have lost my daughter and we shall miss her. But I bear no ill will. I bear no grudge. Dirty sort of talk is not going to bring her back . . . She was a pet. She's dead. She's in heaven and we'll meet again. Don't ask me please for a purpose. I don't have a purpose. I don't have an answer. But I know there has to be a plan. If I didn't think that, I would commit suicide. It's part of a greater plan, and God is good. And we shall meet again.'
>
> I did not use the word 'forgive' in that broadcast, nor in any later one, but people understood that my words were about forgiveness. Our Lord taught us to pray, 'forgive us our sins, as we forgive those who sin against us'. We ask God to forgive us, but we are subject always to his condition that we must forgive others. God's forgiveness is ultimate, ours is the forgiveness of man to man. To me, the two become one. It's as simple as that. My words were not intended as a statement

of theology or of righteousness, rather they were from the heart, and they expressed how I felt at the time, and as I still do.

Gordon Wilson with Alf McCreary

There have been a number of tragedies for which special prayers have been written and special services held. There follow a few examples of such prayers and extracts. Identical occasions are unlikely to happen, but these prayers may be helpful in different but similar circumstances.

The Marchioness *Disaster*

An extract from the service held in Southwark Cathedral after the sinking of the MV Marchioness *on the River Thames in London.*

Introduction

Minister
For about a thousand years this church has stood by the river.
Today it is our privilege to offer what we can in order to share the grief and the prayers of those who mourn after the tragedy of the sinking of the Motor Vessel *Marchioness*. One of the ancient docks near this church is named after St Mary, the mother of Jesus, and today we may recall what was said about her grief: 'A sword shall pierce your heart.'

Another of the old docks on this South Bank of the Thames is named St Saviour's, for this is the church of the Saviour and St Mary. The Saviour is Jesus Christ, who has conquered death and all forms of darkness. Our Lord invited us to accept the eternal light and love of God our Heavenly Father. He says: 'Blessed are those who mourn, for they shall be comforted.'

We entrust into the merciful keeping of God, their Creator, Redeemer and Sanctifier, the souls of those we remember today.

A period of silence is kept for remembrance.

O Father of all, we pray to you for those whom we love,
but see no longer. Grant them your peace; let light perpetual shine upon them; and in your good loving wisdom and almighty power work in them the good purpose of your perfect will, through Jesus Christ our Lord.
Amen.

We pray for those who survive and mourn, that all may know the comfort of God's presence amid grief.

A period of silence is kept for reflection.

Father in heaven, you gave your Son Jesus Christ to suffering and to death on the cross, and raised him to life in glory. Grant us a patient faith in time of darkness, and strengthen our hearts with the knowledge of your love.
Amen.

O Lord, grant us the light of your Spirit, that we may live more bravely and faithfully for your sake and for the sake of those who are no longer with us here on earth; and enable us so to serve you day by day that we may find eternal fellowship with them in you; through him who died and rose again for us all, your Son Jesus Christ, our Saviour. Amen.

'Out of Darkness into Light'

Extracts from a memorial service held in Dunblane Cathedral for the sixteen children and the teacher who died in the Dunblane Primary School tragedy on 13 March 1996.

An Act of Remembrance

Praise

Tune: Melita ('Eternal Father, strong to save')
O Father, on your love we call,
When sorrow overshadows all,
And pain that feels too great to bear
Drives from us any words for prayer;
    Enfold in love for ever more
    All those we love, but see no more.

Our children, innocent and dear,
Were strangers to a world of fear;
Each precious life had more to give,
In each, our hopes and dreams could live;
    Enfold in love for ever more
    All those we love, but see no more.

So brief, the joy since each was born,
So long the years in which to mourn;
Give us compassion to sustain
Each other in this time of pain;
    Enfold in love for ever more
    All those we love, but see no more.

Guard us from bitterness and hate,
And share with us grief's crushing weight;
Help us to live from day to day
Until, once more, we find our way;
    Enfold in love for ever more
    All those we love but see no more.

When dark despair is all around,
And falling tears the only sound,
Light one small flame of hope that still
You walk with us, and always will
Enfold in love for ever more
All those we love, but see no more.

Jean Holloway

Reading – Little child lost

Shall we ever find anything other than a child that can be
such a paradox in our lives? A little person that can generate
such a conflict of anger and love. One that causes so much
disappointment and pride at the same time. So much sorrow
when they have been hurt, only to cause so much happiness
with their laughter.

One who can cause so much fear for their safety and well-being,
cause so much comfort and serenity when they are asleep in your
arms. This little person has the ability to pull at each and every
emotion known to man and some that they are not even aware of.

When the loss of this little person happens, no matter how, what
do we do then? Will we ever escape the sound of their voice;
does it still come from their room?

We will never quit catching a glimpse of them out of the corner of
our eye. Was that my little one or just an illusion? Your answer is –
you see and hear – just as you continue to love, for you see that
child was a part of your soul. Although you may not always hear
them, as they move upon the wings of the wind, nor may you
always see them as they flash past on a ray of sunlight, be assured
they are with you.

Though I may never be able to explain your loss or console you,
I wish to thank you. For you see, without your child, and other
children who have gone before us, there would be no other
children in heaven. Playing where they never tire, your child
is safe and happy.

Eugene G. Merryman Jr
June 1995, France
Copyright © 1995 Ka Ge Co

The Lament

The Piper plays 'Lament for the Children' by Patrick Mor MacCrimmon. A candle is lit for each of the sixteen children and their teacher as we remember their lives.

Remembering the children

Would God that I had died for thee,
O Absalom my son, my son.

2 Samuel 18.33

Truly, I say to you, unless you turn and become like children, you will never enter the kingdom of heaven. Whoever humbles himself like this child, he is the greatest in the kingdom of heaven.

St Matthew 18.3-4

Remembering Gwen Mayor

I will guide you in the way you should go.
I will counsel and watch over you.

Psalm 32.8

Silence is observed for one minute.

The gift of tears

Lord, we give you thanks for the gift of tears:
For tears of grief, redeeming our mourning from despair;
For tears of anger, awakening our thirst for justice;
For tears of laughter, celebrating our joy in living.

May the light of Christ shining through our tears
Become the rainbow of your promise,
Shedding colours of your love's bright presence
In your grieving, struggling, laughing world.

Source unknown

11 September
Terrorist Attacks in the USA

A reading

. . . Where was God
on September the Eleventh? He was begging
in old clothes in the subway
beneath the World Trade Center.
He was homeless in Gaza,
imprisoned in Afghanistan,
running the gauntlet to her school in the Ardoyne,
starving in Somalia,
dying of AIDS in an Angolan slum,
suffering everywhere in this fast-shrinking world;
and boarding a plane unwittingly in Boston,
heading for an appointment on the 110th floor.

When the time came he stretched out his arms
    once more to take
the dreadful impact that would pierce his side.
His last message on his fading cell phone
once more to ask forgiveness for them all, before
his body fell under the weight of so much evil.

Silence is observed.

Godfrey Rust: from the poem 'September 11, 2001'

Service of Commemoration and Remembrance: St Paul's Cathedral, London, 11 September 2002

Intercessions

Eternal and gracious God, hear the prayers of your people
as we remember in sorrow all those who died on this day
in New York, Washington and Pennsylvania.
As we commemorate the precious gift of their lives
we commend them, in faith and trust,
to your embracing love and mercy.

Lord, in your mercy
hear our prayer.

God of all care and compassion, hear our prayer
for each broken family and every broken heart.
Hold them through the pain of grief,
surround them with the gentle care they need
and give them strength for the future that is yet to be.

Lord, in your mercy
hear our prayer.

God of our health and strength,
hear our prayer for those who were injured and hurt.
Give patience and skill to those who look after them
and heal the wounds of body, mind and spirit.

Lord, in your mercy
hear our prayer.

God of life and love, we pray with gratitude
for the bravery and endurance of the emergency services.
Keep in safety those who risk their own lives
to rescue others in danger.

Lord, in your mercy
hear our prayer.

God of wisdom and truth,
we pray for the leaders of the nations;
for wisdom and courage in those who stand firm
     against terrorism;
for patience and persistence in all who work
to secure freedom, justice and peace on earth.

Lord, in your mercy
hear our prayer.

God of mercy, we pray for peoples and nations bleeding still
from the unhealed wounds of their history.
Deliver them from violence and vengeance;
nurture in them the ancient wisdom of respect
     and mutual understanding.

Lord, in your mercy
hear our prayer.

God of time and eternity, you travel with us
     through deep waters,
yet never abandon us in the storm.
We live still in darkened days, yet never without
     your healing light.
Renew our confidence, rekindle our hope, deepen our faith,
guide us in truth and give us peace in our day.

Lord, in your mercy
hear our prayer.

Merciful Father of all,
in darkness and in light,
in trouble and in joy,
in death and in life,
help us to trust your love,
to serve your purpose
and to praise your name for ever.

The Bishop
Together with those who have gathered in New York,
Washington, Pennsylvania and countless people around the
world, we remember those who died at this time, on this
day, one year ago.

Act of Remembrance

Sophie Brandt, September 11 Programme Officer,
British Red Cross
Time is too slow for those who wait,
too swift for those who fear,
too long for those who grieve,
too short for those who rejoice,
but for those who love, time is eternity.
Henry Van Dyke (1852–1933)

The Bishop
With the stirring of the wind and the chill of winter,
under the blue sky and in the warmth of summer,
We remember them.

With joys we long to share and in sorrow we bear alone;
In work we have to do with life we have to give,
We remember them.

In treasured memories of the past
and during days to come
We remember them.

In all that they achieved and for all that might have been;
at the dawn of day and in the setting sun
We remember them.

Silence is kept, during which more than three thousand rose petals are released from the Whispering Gallery.

The Minor Canon

If I should die and leave you here awhile,
Be not like others, sore undone, who keep
Long vigils by the silent dust, and weep.
For my sake, turn again to life and smile,
Nerving thy heart and trembling hand to do
Something to comfort weaker hearts than thine
And I perchance may therein comfort you.

A. Price Hughes

A Service of Remembrance for all who died in Iraq: St Paul's Cathedral, London, 10 October 2003

The Bidding

We come to this cathedral today from all parts of this nation to remember before God all who have died in Iraq in the course of the hostilities this year.

We pray especially for all servicemen and women from the United Kingdom who have lost their lives or who have suffered injury, and with them we remember their families, their colleagues and their friends.

We continue to hold before God all who are still on active service in Iraq; we pray for their well-being and for all who hold them in their hearts at home.

We give thanks for all who work for peace, for freedom, for justice, for the Armed Services; for the emergency services; for all who carry the burdens of government.

We bring before God in penitence the hatreds of our world, the deep divisions of our humanity. We ask for a new understanding, a new resolve, a new obedience to the law of love. We pray for peace.

And we pray in particular for Iraq, and for all who work in the face of great danger day by day to establish peace and security and the well-being of all its people.

And so we come from many places, from different traditions of faith, to unite in thanksgiving, in remembrance, in prayer before God, as we say together:

Our Father, etc.

Prayers for penitence and reconciliation

We turn to God in sorrow as we acknowledge before him
the suffering of his world and the pain of his people.

When hatred causes divisions between nations
and alienates races and cultures,
Lord, have mercy.
Lord, have mercy.

When indifference diminishes the dignity
of the imprisoned, the homeless and the refugee,
Christ, have mercy.
Christ, have mercy.

When pride leads us to trust ourselves and to disregard
the demands of your word and your laws,
Lord, have mercy.
Lord, have mercy.

May God, who has called us to be kind to one another,
tender-hearted and forgiving of one another, pour upon us
the riches of his grace, free us from evil, and strengthen us
to live in love and peace with all the peoples of the earth.
Amen.

Let us then pray with hope for the future of the world:
for peace on earth and goodwill among all people;
for an end to injustice, terrorism and war;
and for those charged with building the ways of peace.
God of mercy
hear our prayer.

For the unity of all Christian people
and for people of faith in every land;
for all who seek God and the way of truth,
God of mercy
hear our prayer.

For the healing of memories,
for relief where past wrongs and violence persist,
and for all who are in pain and distress,
God of mercy
hear our prayer.

For the strengthening of the bonds of human dignity,
for the resolve of all whose courage and compassion
    bring relief,
and for those who, day by day,
meet hostility with restraint,
God of mercy
hear our prayer.

For those striving to keep peace in Iraq,
for their continued professionalism, commitment
    and bravery,
and for the safety of all those
rebuilding the fabric of life,
God of mercy
hear our prayer.

For friendship and trust among all,
that we might discern more deeply our shared humanity,
and for the dawning of a world that is
in harmony with itself,
God of mercy
hear our prayer.

O God, look in mercy
on the deep divisions of our world.
Set in our hearts the spirit of penitence,
forgiveness and reconciliation,
that the day may soon come when we no longer distrust
or fear one another, but are drawn together
in unity of purpose, in understanding,
and in love; through Jesus Christ, our Lord.
Amen.

Madrid Madness

Commuters start another day,
ordinary in their anonymity,
fatigued by the ritual of routine,
not staring strangers in the eye.

7.39 a.m.
11.03.04,
platforms thronged,
workers jostle,
children scramble,
lovers part,
parents squabble.

7.45 a.m.
11.03.04,
the silence of the dead
shatters the Spanish day;
as terror rips open
the heart of a nation,
and evil boards a
train from the depths of hell.

Atocha,
El Pozo,
Santa Eugenia,
destination points
on a journey of grief and mourning,
travelled by those innocent
of all crime except living.

People scream
and rush for safety,
running away from terror
into tunnels of fear.
Blasts burst open the sky
like a beast gone wild.
Madness beyond all reckoning
visits Madrid in black cruelty.

Railway carriages thrown up into death;
chaos rushes in to replace timetabled order;
the struggle of rescue begins,
horror witnessed by those numbed in shock.

Bodies beyond remembering,
limbs separated from belonging,
lives crushed out of loving,
evil beyond all imagining.

Unknown strangers now locked together
in an eternal embrace of horror;
bodies lined up in a parody of waiting
on platforms of no future departing.

Evil oozes out of humanity's flesh,
and takes root in the bitter soil of hatred.
Suspicion lurks around the streets,
as the world murmurs its opinion.

There has to be another way;
as love demonstrates against fear,
peace marches the road of pain,
as thousands cry for justice.

Madrid
7.39 a.m.
11.03.04;
a litany of destruction,
as life extinguished
by remote terror;
cries out for purpose,
shouts out for an end
to all horror of this kind.

Donald Macaskill

Jessica Chapman and Holly Wells

Jessica Chapman and Holly Wells were murdered in Soham
in August 2002. At the memorial service held for them in Ely
Cathedral the Vicar of Soham, the Revd Tim Alban Jones, said:

In the course of their short lives Holly and Jessica achieved about
the same as most ten-year-olds – perhaps just a little more – but in
their deaths they have certainly achieved more than any of us will
manage in our lifetime.

In the course of the past two weeks we have witnessed the most
extraordinary sights: we have seen thousands upon thousands of
flowers, cards, and soft toys being brought to St Andrew's Church
in memory of Jessica and Holly; we have seen strangers and
friends weeping together in shared grief and anguish; we have
seen the dedication and diligence of hundreds of police officers;
we have seen our town of Soham brought together and united in
a common grief; and we have seen the extraordinary bravery and
courage of two families . . .

In our reading from St Paul's first letter to the Early Church in
Corinth, a reading that is so very familiar to many of us, St Paul is
telling those first Christians all about the love of God, which has
been revealed in the person of Jesus. In our lives many of us are
privileged to know something of that love of God through our
dealings with one another. Holly and Jessica were both loving
children . . . They were brought up to know and treasure the value
of love . . . In all our recent sadness we have still been able to
catch glimpses of the love of God at work in the world through
the generosity of people in their sympathy, love and support . . .
But perhaps for the girls' families there is some comfort in the
knowledge that in the love of God as shown in Jesus there is
unbroken continuity from this world to the next.

And what of the future? Where do we go from here? . . . We must
not raise our children to live in an atmosphere of constant fear and
suspicion, where everyone is mistrusted. Of course there are risks
in this way, and society needs to take every possible step to
eliminate or reduce those risks. We need to make sure that the
trust and love we teach our children is not misused or betrayed.
But I am convinced that the way forward is the way of openness

and trust, not the way of fear and suspicion. We need to let
our lives be ruled by love and goodness, not hate and deeds of
darkness. The witness of the many flowers outside St Andrew's
Church, the huge number of cards of support, testifies eloquently
to the power of love and goodness. They show ultimately that
the power of love is stronger, far stronger, than the works of
wickedness. The darkness may seem to win for a while, but
in the end light and goodness will prevail.

In Pilgrim Post, *the Bulletin of Churches Together in England,
the Revd Alan Ashton, the Superintendent Minister of the
Newmarket Methodist Circuit, which includes Soham, wrote:*

It soon became apparent that the Community needed the Church
and not denominations . . . Our denominations were washed
away by the needs of our community and those who started
arriving in their thousands to lay flowers, light a Candle of Love
and sign the Book of Condolence.

So as Churches Together, along with the needs of Soham, we
hoped, grieved and prayed together. We have not yet faced
forgiveness – perhaps some never will be able to do so – but
as such a vital part of our Gospel proclamation we must face
the issues it raises with the community, and we must seek to
do so together in Christ when the time is right.

> O God who brought us to birth
> And in whose arms we die:
> In our grief and shock
> Contain and comfort us;
> Embrace us with your love,
> Give us hope in our confusion,
> And grace to let go into new life,
> Through Jesus Christ, Amen.

Janet Morley

Hymns and Music

Song of farewell

Words: ICEL
Music: Gerry Fitzpatrick

We cannot measure how you heal

Words: John Bell and Graham Maule; The Iona Community
Tune: 'Ye banks and braes', Scots traditional, arranged JLB

Gently

We can - not meas - ure how you heal or

an - swer ev - ery suf - ferer's prayer, yet

we be - lieve your grace re - sponds where

faith__ and doubt u - nite to care. Your

We cannot measure how you heal
Or answer every sufferer's prayer,
Yet we believe your grace responds
Where faith and doubt unite to care.
Your hands, though blooded on the cross,
Survive to hold and heal and warn,
To carry all through death to life
And cradle children yet unborn.

The pain that will not go away,
The guilt that clings from things long past,
The fear of what the future holds,
Are present as if meant to last.
But present too is love that tends
The hurt we never hoped to find,
The private agonies inside,
The memories that haunt the mind.

So some have come who need your help
And some have come to make amends,
As hands which shaped and saved the world
Are present in the touch of friends.
Lord, let your Spirit meet us here
To mend the body, mind and soul,
To disentangle peace from pain
And make your broken people whole.

Index of First Lines

O Lord, grant us the light of your Spirit, 86
One ever hangs where shelled roads part, 19
Our Father in heaven, 52, 65

Receive his/her soul, 102
Remember what you will, 36
Risen Jesus, we thank you for your greeting, 24
Risen, reigning Christ, 30

Say 'no' to peace, 22

The desert will sing and rejoice, 43
The God of peace fill you with all joy, 46, 66
The God of peace, who brought again from the dead, 46
The grace of our Lord Jesus Christ, 45
The peace of God, which passes all understanding, 46
These hearts were woven of human joys and cares, 17
They are not here. And we, we are the Others, 20
Thus says the Lord: A voice in Ramah, 78
Time is too slow for those who wait, 93

Under his helmet, up against his pack, 18

We believe in God, God the Holy One, 43
We believe God made this world, 41
We believe in God, who made the sun and the sky, 42
We believe in Jesus Christ, 41
We cannot measure how you heal, 105
We had forgotten You, or very nearly, 16
We look forward with hope, 44
What shall we pray for those who died, 49
Where there is war and conflict, 26
Where was God on September the Eleventh?, 90
With proud thanksgiving, a mother for her children, 15
With the stirring of the wind and the chill of winter, 93

You raise the dead to life in the spirit, 54